D1528901

RBI—An Anecdotal History

ABOUT THE AUTHOR

P.P. Ramachandran, 78 years old, is a Post graduate in Economics, Post graduate in Comparative Mythology, Certificate and Diploma holder in Sanskrit from Mumbai University. He has served in the Reserve Bank of India for forty years in a number of Departments and retired as Deputy General Manager. He writes for several journals and is a prolific reviewer of books, a book selector for Libraries. He gives lectures regularly to audiences, young and old on different disciplines. He resides in Mumbai with his wife and two daughters. He is a rare bird—a literary banker. His hobbies are reading, writing and watching English, Malayalam movies and art-films. He has published one book: "A Bunch of Fragrant Roses" (Academic Foundation).

RBI—An Anecdotal History

P.P. RAMACHANDRAN

ACADEMIC FOUNDATION
NEW DELHI

www.academicfoundation.org

First published in 2016
by

ACADEMIC FOUNDATION
4772-73 / 23 Bharat Ram Road, (23 Ansari Road),
Darya Ganj, New Delhi - 110 002 (India).
Phones : 23245001 / 02 / 03 / 04.
Fax : +91-11-23245005.
E-mail : books@academicfoundation.com
www.academicfoundation.org

Disclaimer:
The opinions/views/findings expressed in this book are solely those of the
author and do not necessarily reflect the views of the publisher.

RBI—An Anecdotal History

By P.P. Ramachandran

ISBN 9789332703117

Typeset by Italics India, New Delhi.
Printed and bound by The Book Mint, New Delhi.
www.thebookmint.in

Contents

This book is humbly dedicated to my parents
my father, Shri P.V. Parameswaran, a great teacher, a grand scholar and an impressive singer. A man of true culture whose impact on me has been phenomenal and my Mother Smt Ananthalakshmy, a very pious person.

Foreword

PPR, as we all affectionately call Shri P.P. Ramachandran, is one person you can always count on when you want stories and anecdotes of persons in or connected with RBI. He is thus a favourite at farewell functions. He has an amazing memory which he calls upon at such events.

He is also the person who keeps close track of events in the lives of RBIites and always lets us know when they say farewell to this world! Furthermore, in his unique way, he got the RBI Governor to honour the centenarian Nair in Kochi. It is therefore, fitting that he has brought out his second book on "An Anecdotal History of RBI".

History, it is said, is drab without it helping us to understand why events took the course they did, who the persons were behind the events and the decisions shaping those events and why those persons took the decisions they did. What was the interaction between those at the top in RBI, the political leadership, the bureaucracy and industry? What were their personal preferences and prejudices? These are questions that you and I would like to get answers for, but invariably do not.

His pen portraits of the 23 Governors of RBI are fascinating and in few pages he has taken us through the history of the 80 year old lady of Mint Street.

In this book, PPR has given us some insight to the personal aspects of the folks in RBI and some anecdotes from their lives. I was quite amused to read a story of the temper of a grand uncle of mine PVR who worked in RBI and was apparently quite a legend!

He has been a popular reviewer of books written by former RBI staff especially Governors and Deputy Governors and he has included many of the important reviews that have been published in this collection.

I am sure the reader would enjoy PPR's book as much as I did.

—Usha Thorat
Former Deputy Governor
Reserve Bank of India.

Preface

The former Reserve Bank of India Deputy (RBI) Governor Shri S.S.Tarapore, in a letter to me wrote: "I am deeply impressed by your fantastic memory of anecdotes and events during your stint in the RBI. As you appreciate the records do not carry the anecdotal aspects of the RBI History. I would suggest that your anecdotes and analysis could be published...."

This book is the result of that inspiring message as also the perseverance with which my wife Lakshmy has egged me on night and day. I have spent four long decades in the RBI and worked under 16 Governors from the second Indian Governor Shri Benegal Rama Rau to Dr C. Rangarajan. I have been recounting at different fora anecdotes and stories about Reserve Bank. My reviews of over 45 books connected with RBI or written by RBI Executives have won plaudits from several Governors and Deputy Governors.

I have had the close support of my family and good friends in this effort. The 'Imp in my life', my Grandson Ashish Gopal has helped me overcome my all-too-common computer glitches.

I express my deep gratitude to Smt Usha Thorat, former Deputy Governor who readily acceded to my request and gave an affectionate "Foreword" to my book.

Last but not the least, my thanks flow to Shri Rituraj Kapila , Academic Foundation, who has published my second book and has been my friend, guide and philosopher throughout this project.

— P.P. Ramachandran.

PART-I

Introduction

The origins of the Reserve Bank of India (RBI) is traceable to the year 1926 when the Royal Commission on Indian Currency and Finance—commonly known as the Hilton-Young Commission—recommended the creation of a Central Bank for India in order to separate the control of currency and credit from the government and augment banking facilities throughout the country. The Reserve Bank of India Act of 1934 established the RBI and set in motion a series of measures culminating in the start of operations in 1935. Since then, the RBI's role and functions have undergone significant changes keeping pace with alterations in the complexion of the nation's economy and its financial sector.

Starting as a private shareholders' bank, the RBI was nationalised in 1949. It then assumed the responsibility to meet the aspirations of a newly independent country and its people. The Reserve Bank's nationalisation aimed at achieving coordination between the policies of the government and those of the Central Bank.

The Preamble to the Reserve Bank of India Act 1934, under which it was constituted, specifies it's objective----"to regulate the issue of Bank notes and the keeping of reserves with a view to securing monetary stability in India and generally to operate the currency and credit system of the country to its advantage." Almost 80 years later, the Bank has taken on different functions keeping pace with altered national interests and global developments.

The core function of the Bank has been to adopt a monetary policy with the main objectives of maintaining price stability and guaranteeing credit flow to essential sectors in the economy. Financial stability too has acquired importance. The Bank's activities guarantee people access to the banking system and maintenance of overall health of the financial system. The Bank's umbrella now covers banking institutions, cooperative banks, regional rural banks, development financial institutions and non-banking financial companies.

Foreign exchange reserves are of paramount importance and the RBI has been closely monitoring this under Defence of India rules, the Foreign Exchange Regulation Act 1947 and the Foreign Exchange Management Act 1999.

With the beginning of an era of planned development RBI's role underwent a sea-change and included developmental functions to encourage savings and capital formation as well as to support widening and deepening of the agricultural and industrial set-up.

As years advanced, RBI adopted international best practices in areas such as prudential regulation, banking technology, variety of monetary policy instruments, external sector management and currency management with a view to make its new policy framework successful.

PART-II

Twenty Three Governors: A Brief Peep

I.   Governor Sir Osborne Arkell Smith
(01-04-1935 to 30-06-1937)

Two striking aspects about the 1st Governor of RBI are that Sir Osborne Smith did not sign any banknote; and that he resigned before his term of office of three and half years was over.

He was a professional banker who served for over 20 years with the Bank of New South Wales, Australia's largest trading bank and 10 years with the Commonwealth Bank of Australia, which undertook both commercial and central banking functions. He came to India in 1926 as a Managing Governor of the Imperial Bank of India. His stewardship of the Imperial Bank won him recognition in banking circles in India.

He was selected by the legendary Montagu Norman, Governor of the Bank of England who wanted "a person on whom the Bank of England could rely and of whom they would expect unquestioning cooperation." Smith took office on 1 April 1935 but he had a short term—he resigned in October 1936. The reasons for the Governor's resignation have not been explained in the official history of RBI. The recently released *James Taylor Papers*, throws a flood of light on 'Smith's murky exit.'

Smith had a regular battle with the Finance Member, Sir James Grigg. Also, there was no love lost with his Deputy Governor, James Taylor. Smith's financial dealings were questioned by his adversaries.

Allegations were made of a scandalous liaison with the wife of an RBI Officer. This was conduct unbecoming of an RBI Governor! The charges against Smith related not only to his technical competence, but also to his character, views and temperament.

According to C.D. Deshmukh, "Smith's temperamental incompatibilty with James Grigg and James Taylor, the serious difference of opinion which arose between him and the Finance Member over the lowering of the Bank Rate, with all its implications and the management of the Bank's investments were the cause of Smith's resignation."

Relations between the Governor and his Deputy Taylor had deteriorated so much that the two took pains to avoid each other. The Finance Member had tapped the Governor's phone and intercepted his mail and that of his alleged mistress!

Smith has another dubious distinction. He had not signed a currency note. Actually he had signed one but that was not issued because of the abdication of Edward VIII. Another story of 'the heart has its reasons'! Sir Osborne Smith was knighted in 1929 and further conferred a Knight Commander of the Indian Empire (KCIE) in 1932.

II.   Governor Sir James Braid Taylor
(01-07-1937 to 17-02-1943)

Sir James Braid Taylor was the 2nd Governor of the RBI, holding office from 1 July 1937, until his death on 17 February 1943. He succeeded Sir Osborne Smith who was the Governor from 1 April 1935 to 30 June 1937. Taylor, a member of the Indian Civil Service, served as a Deputy Controller in the Currency Department of the Government of India (GoI) for over a decade. He later became the Controller of Currency, and Additional Secretary in the Finance Department. He was appointed as the Deputy Governor of RBI and eventually succeeded Osborne Smith as the Governor. He was closely associated with the preparation and piloting of the RBI Bill. The task of planning the organisation and administration of the RBI was entrusted to Sir

James, whose knowledge about the details of administration was extraordinarily close. He saw the Bank through the war years and the financial experiments that were engendered and catalysed, including the decision to move from a silver currency to fiat money. Even though he was the second Governor, his signature was the first to appear on the currency notes of the Indian rupee. His second term came to an end when he died in office on 17 February 1943. He was succeeded by Sir C.D. Deshmukh who became the first Indian to lead the RBI.

Relations between Governor Osborne Smith and Deputy Governor James Taylor were not quite cordial. The Governor suspected that Sir James Taylor wrote to GoI without informing him. A stage was reached when Taylor threatened to resign if Smith returned from England (he was there on a visit). James Grigg, the Finance Member, threatened to resign if Taylor did. Smith was eased out and wrote in a letter, "My God! How I would love to smack the Viceroy, Grigg, Taylor and all concerned".

Taylor hailed from the Central Province (CP) and Berar services, but was transferred to the Centre where his financial abilities received early recognition. Taylor strongly espoused C.D. Deshmukh and arranged for Deshmukh's attachment to the Bank of England so that he could get the feel of central banking.

During Taylor's tenure, the RBI's accounting year was changed from January-December to July-June in March 1940.

Taylor died on 17 February 1943, due to coronary thrombosis, pneumonia and cardiac failure. Among the pall bearers was C.D. Deshmukh. According to Deshmukh,

> Sir James Taylor was among the most remarkable man that has been my good fortune to know. His intelligence is like a lambent flame which illumined everything that it touched and purged it of dross and he had a catholicity of interest, a breadth of outlook and a warm humanity which I have seldom seen equalled.

In the British Civil Services Examination of 1913, James Grigg stood first and James Taylor second. James Taylor was appointed a

Companion of the Indian Empire (CIE) in the 1933 New Year Honours List, knighted in the 1935 Silver Jubilee and Birthday Honours List and further appointed a KCIE in the 1939 Birthday Honours List.

III.   Governor Sir C.D. Deshmukh
(11-08-1943 to 30-06-1949)

Chintaman Dwarkanath Deshmukh, a member of the Indian Civil Service (ICS) was the first Indian Governor of the Bank. His association with the Bank commenced in 1939, when he was appointed the government's Liaison Officer. He later served as Secretary and thereafter in 1941 as Deputy Governor of the Bank. On the demise of James Taylor, he took over stewardship of the Bank, and was appointed Governor in August 1943.

During his tenure as Governor, he represented India at the Bretton Woods negotiations in 1944, saw the transition to Independence and the partition of the country and the division of assets and liabilities of the Reserve Bank between India and Pakistan. He helped the smooth transition of the Bank from a shareholders' institution to a state-owned organisation, when the institution was nationalised on 1 January 1949.

Chintaman Deshmukh had an outstanding educational career. He stood first in the Matriculation examination of the University of Bombay in 1912, and also secured the first Jagannath Sankersett Scholarship in Sanskrit. At the University of Cambridge in 1917, he graduated in the field of Natural Sciences Tripos with Botany, Chemistry and Geology, winning the Frank Smart Prize in Botany. He appeared for the ICS Examination in 1918, then held only in London and topped the list of successful candidates.

For most of his 21 years with the ICS, Deshmukh was with the then CP and Berar Government. While on leave in London, he worked as one of the secretaries to the Second Round Table Conference in which

Mahatma Gandhi had participated. The memorandum submitted by the CP and Berar government, which Deshmukh had prepared for the purpose of the enquiry by Sir Otto Niemeyer leading to an award on the financial relations between the Centre and the Provinces under the Government of India Act 1935, won him high acclaim.

His association with the RBI began in July 1939, when he was appointed Liaison Officer in the Bank in order to keep the GoI in touch with the institution's affairs. Three months later, he was appointed Secretary of the Central Board of the Bank and two years later in December 1941, as the Deputy Governor. He was Governor from 11 August 1943 to 30 June 1949.

Deshmukh proved to be an outstanding Governor. He secured the enactment of a comprehensive legislation for the regulation of banking companies and the establishment of the first financial institution for the provision of long-term credit to industry, namely the Industrial Finance Corporation of India (IFCI). He also initiated a number of steps for building an adequate machinery for rural credit.

Deshmukh played an important role in the Bretton Woods Conference in July 1944, which led to the establishment of the International Monetary Fund (IMF) and International Bank for Reconstruction and Development (IBRD). In both of these institutions, Deshmukh was a Member of the Board of Governors for 10 years and was the Chairman at their Joint Annual Meeting held in Paris in 1950.

Towards the end of 1949, Jawaharlal Nehru asked Deshmukh to work on organisation of the Planning Commission and appointed him as its member while setting up on 1 April 1950. Shortly thereafter, he joined the Union Cabinet as the Finance Minister and held that office with distinction until he resigned in July 1956. He was also primarily responsible for important landmarks in the area of social control, such as the enactment of a new Companies Act, and nationalisation of the Imperial Bank of India and life insurance companies.

A different phase of public service by Deshmukh in the realms of education and social service was noticed since his Chairmanship of the University Grants Commission (UGC) from 1956 to 1960, helping to lay a solid foundation for the improvement of the standards of university education in the country. He was Vice-Chancellor of the University of Delhi from March 1962 to February 1967, building it up as an outstanding institution for higher learning.

Deshmukh was President of the Indian Statistical Institute (ISI) from 1945 to 1964. It was during the period when he was both the President of the ISI and the Union Finance Minister when the National Sample Survey (NSS), to be conducted by the ISI, was instituted (1951-52), and the Central Statistics Office was established.

Deshmukh's old college at Cambridge, Jesus College, elected him an Honorary Fellow in 1952. He was co-recipient of the Ramon Magsaysay Foundation Award for distinguished government service in 1959, as also at the ISI.

He had a great love for gardening, and horticulture was his special hobby. His love for Sanskrit is well known and he published a volume of his poems in Sanskrit in 1969. He had translated Kalidasa's *Meghadutham* into Marathi. He was also proficient in a number of foreign languages.

Deshmukh held the office of Union Finance Minister from 1950 until 1956, when the Central Government reorganised the Indian states on a linguistic basis.

He was first married to an English woman through whom he had a daughter; this marriage ended when his wife returned to England and his attempt at reconciliation in 1946 failed. He later married Durgabai Deshmukh who was a childless widow, a freedom fighter, and a member of the Congress Party.

In 1974, he published his autobiography, *The Course Of My Life*.

In 1937, Deshmukh was appointed a CIE. The British Government conferred a knighthood upon Deshmukh in 1944. In 1975, the GoI honoured Deshmukh with a Padma Vibhushan award.

IV. **Governor Sir Benegal Rama Rau**
(01-07-1949 to 14-01-1957)

Sir Benegal Rama Rau was the fourth Governor of the RBI. He was educated at Presidency College, Madras, and at Kings College, Cambridge. Joining the ICS in 1919, he was appointed a CIE in 1930, and was knighted in 1939. He had the longest tenure as Governor of the RBI, which was cut short when he resigned prior to the expiry of his second extended term, due to differences with Shri T.T. Krishnamachari (TTK), the Finance Minister.

On joining the ICS and before joining the RBI, he held the following posts: Under-Secretary and Deputy Secretary to the Government of Madras, Finance Department as Secretary to the Indian Taxation Committee, Finance Department as Deputy Secretary, Simon Commission as Financial Adviser, Industries Department Joint Secretary, Round Table Conference as Secretary, Deputy High Commissioner for India in London, High Commissioner for India in South Africa. When he returned to India, he was appointed Chairman of the Bombay Port Trust. After serving the post, he once again served as a diplomat in form of the Indian Ambassador to Japan, and the Ambassador to the United States (US). His last position was as the Governor of the RBI.

The events that marked his tenure at the Reserve Bank included: the devaluation of the rupee in 1949 consequent to the identical devaluation of the pound sterling; commencement of the planning era, innovative cooperative credit and industrial finance initiatives; and importantly, the recommendations of the All India Rural Credit Survey Committee paving the way for nationalisation of the Imperial Bank of India in order to form the State Bank of India (SBI).

According to the *Reserve Bank History-Volume II*, events in 1956-57 culminated in Rama Rau's resignation as Governor directly as a result of the disagreements with Finance Minister TTK, which in turn erupted into barely concealed conflict late in 1956. According to Rama Rau, TTK had exhibited "personal rudeness", used "very rude language", passed "rude remarks" and indulged in "rude behaviour." The FM spoke derogatorily to the Governor of RBI as "a department or "section" of the Finance Ministry. In the Parliament, TTK accused the Bank of being "reserved" as well as "incapable of doing any positive thinking."

What proved to be the last straw was the announcement by TTK of a stamp duty on bills. TTK wanted money to continue to be cheap, but at the same time said the tax, which would eventually raise the lending rate, was a credit control measure. Rama Rau and others tried to dissuade TTK, but to no avail. TTK even told the Parliament that the proposed hike was a "fiscal measure with a monetary intent"! This led Rama Rau to write a letter stating that henceforth, "two authorities would operate the Bank Rate." The matter went up to Jawaharlal Nehru, and a meeting was called in the cabinet room to discuss the matter. TTK and Rama Rau came face to face outside it, and according to B.K. Nehru, TTK had "let fly in no uncertain terms and in the loudest of voices." He made it clear that the RBI was a "department" or "section" of the finance ministry.

In 1957, Benegal Rama Rau, the fourth and longest serving RBI Governor resigned from his post, accusing the then Finance Minister TTK of interference.

Sir Rama Rau's elder brother, Sir Benegal Narsing Rau was an Indian civil servant, jurist, diplomat and statesman known for his key role in drafting the Constitution of India; and his younger brother, B. Shiva Rao became a journalist and politician. Rama Rau was married to Dhanvanthi Rama Rau, a Kashmiri Brahmin, a leader in the Indian women's rights movement and also the International President of Planned Parenthood. Their younger daughter, Santha Rama Rau became a travel writer and settled in the US.

Shri Rama Rau was conferred the CIE by the British Government.

V.   Governor Shri K.G. Ambegaonkar
      (14-01-1957 to 28-02-1957)

Following Sir Benegal Rama Rau's resignation, Shri K.G. Ambegaonkar was appointed as the 5th Governor of RBI and officiated from 14 January 1957 to 28 February 1957, until Shri H.V.R. Iengar could take over as Governor on 1 March 1957. Ambegaonkar was a member of the ICS. He was the Secretary of the Department of Economic Affairs of the Finance Ministry, prior to his appointment as Deputy Governor. He had also served the Bank in senior capacities as the first Officer-in-Charge of the Agricultural Department. He was responsible for putting up proposals for legislation on the improvement of the credit delivery system for agricultural finance and for bringing about a closer connection between agricultural enterprise and the operations of RBI.

K.G. Ambegaonkar did not sign any bank notes.

VI.   Governor Shri H.V.R. Iengar
       (01-03-1957 to 28-02-1962)

H.V.R. Iengar was the 6th Governor of the RBI. He was a member of the ICS. Iengar earned a special niche as a resolute Home Secretary under the redoubtable Sardar Patel. He served as the Chairman of SBI, before his appointment as the Governor of the RBI. After retiring as Governor, he was Chairman of E.I.D. Parry and director in several companies.

During his tenure, the RBI pro-actively supported efforts towards rapid industrialisation of the country and consolidation of the banking sector. Introduction of Deposit Insurance Corporation in India in 1962 was one of the earliest experiments made worldwide in this field. Indian coinage system was shifted from the earlier pies and annas system to decimal coinage. The use of variable cash reserve ratio, along with selective credit control instruments, marked the monetary policy formulation during his time.

In 2002 on his birth centenary, an illustrated book, *Snapshots of History—Through the Writings of H.V.R. Iengar*, consisting of articles, was compiled and edited by his daughter Indira and son-in-law Bipin Patel. The book is lavishly illustrated and carries a number of articles that Iengar wrote after his retirement in 1962. They deal with the events leading to Independence and soon thereafter. The language is elegant and direct, and a delight to read. Clarity of thought, married to precise expression, makes for a book that can be read in one sitting. A wide variety of subjects have been covered, ranging from the last days of the *Raj*, the ICS officers, British and Indian, like Iengar himself, to the relations between the politicians and bureaucrats, the President and Prime Minister.

With prescience he wrote in his article of 15 August 1966:

> I foresee a time when there may be political turmoil and confusion at the Centre in India—shifting loyalties and unstable governments. It is a matter of importance that India has an exceptionally strong civil service, something that the French have evolved... Such a service can keep the country on an even keel.

Another telling quote from his article of 10 December 1966, is: "How can the younger generation dream dreams, when the men in authority cling to power, fight for power and spend their energy in shabby quarrels while hunger stalks the land?"

Iengar was a Professor in the Royal Institute of Science, Bombay. However, he opted for the ICS. After a grilling interview with a retired British civilian, he was asked by the latter, "How do you happen to have three initials when most of the Indians seem content with two?" He had replied, "Sir, my first name, Haravu is a place name in my native Mysore; the second is my personal name which was my granny's choice and a mystified school clerk who was unable to grapple with Varadaraja, split it into Varada Raja."

According to *RBI History-Volume II*,

> Iengar was, by every account, a man of enormous charm and intelligence who brought a keen intellect and abundant energy to

bear on his endeavours. A good listener, he was affable, accessible and encouraged debate within the organisation. Iengar was also effective and vigorous as Governor.

Highly informal in attitude, he initiated the practice of sending for junior officers, who had drafted policy papers and discussing those with them in a totally relaxed manner. He had intense intellectual curiosity and possibly was the only Governor to borrow and read books from the RBI Library. S.L.N. Simha—who was associated with him for two decades neatly summed up Iengar:

> He was an outstanding personality—brilliant as a student, extraordinarily competent as a civil servant, a great Governor of the country's central bank, a very successful company chairman, a superb speaker and a genial person. He was a master of the art of management.

He received the Padma Vibhushan, India's second highest civilian honour in 1962.

VII. Governor Shri P.C. Bhattacharyya
(01-03-1962 to 30-06-1967)

Paresh Chandra Bhattacharyya was the 7th Governor of the RBI from 1 March 1962 to 30 June 1967. Unlike his predecessors, he was a member of the Indian Audit and Accounts Service (IA&AS). He served as Secretary in the Finance Ministry and later as Chairman of the SBI, before his appointment as the Governor.

As RBI Governor, he strongly opposed the nationalising of private banks in India by writing a letter to the then Deputy Prime Minister Morarji Desai, warning about the costs of nationalising the banks asserting that it was not desirable. During his tenure, the currency notes of denomination 5, 10 and 100 was reduced in size. While this was done for economic reasons, lowering the cost of paper and of printing, it also helped in bringing the notes to a handy size.

During his regime, three of the India's biggest financial institutions took shape—the Industrial Development Bank of India (IDBI) in 1964; the Agricultural Finance Corporation in 1963; and the Unit Trust of India (UTI) in 1964. Other developments were introduction of the Credit Authorisation Scheme as an instrument of credit regulation. The devaluation of the Rupee in 1966 to maintain export competitiveness of the economy was a historic event during his era.

According to *RBI History-Volume I*:

> ...Bhattacharyya was self-effacing by temperament but firm when it mattered ..His tenure coincided with the pursuit of a more active monetary policy. He shared a good working relationship with three Finance Ministers—Morarji Desai, T.T. Krishnamachari and Sachindra Chaudhuri.... Krishnamachari's return to the Finance Ministry in August 1963 accelerated the pace of institutional development with startling suddenness and the Bank under Bhattacharya's leadership effectively complemented TTK's initiative to set up institutions such as the IDBI and the Unit Trust.

VIII.   Governor Shri Lakshmi Kant Jha
   (01-07-1967 to 03-05-1970)

Shri Lakshmi Kant Jha was the 8th Governor of the RBI. He graduated from Benaras Hindu University and Trinity College, Cambridge, the United Kingdom (UK). At Cambridge, he was a student of renowned economists like A.C. Pigou, J.M. Keynes and D.H. Robertson and of Harold J. Laski in the LSE. He joined the ICS in 1936. He worked successively as Deputy Secretary in the Supply Department, Chief Controller of Imports and Exports, Joint Secretary in the Ministry of Commerce and Industry and as Secretary, Ministry of Heavy Industry. He was India's Principal Representative at the meetings of the General Agreement on Tariffs and Trade (GATT) and was its Chairman (1957-58). He became Secretary, Department of Economic Affairs in the Ministry of Finance in 1960 and was appointed in 1964 to the newly-created post of Principal Secretary to the then Prime Minister,

Lal Bahadur Shastri. Subsequently, he continued in the same capacity under Prime Minister Indira Gandhi.

He was Governor during one of the most challenging phases of the Indian economy. Food security was a major concern of those times and new initiatives such as the Green Revolution emerged from such concerns. Introduction of social control was the most important milestone in 1968 and in pursuit of this, 14 major commercial banks were nationalised in 1969. His tenure also saw the establishment of National Credit Council (NCC), and the introduction of Lead Bank Scheme to facilitate credit delivery. Amongst other developments, gold controls were brought on a statutory basis; deposit insurance was in principle extended to cooperative banks; and the Agricultural Credit Board was set up.

During his tenure, rupee notes of the denominations of 2, 5, 10, and 100, commemorating the birth centenary of Mahatma Gandhi, were released on 2 October 1969; these notes bear his signature, both in English and Hindi. The signature in Hindi, the official language of the GoI, appeared on the currency notes for the first time during his stewardship of the RBI.

He was a many-sided personality who excelled in several walks of life. He was an eminent economist, a distinguished administrator, an able diplomat and a sage counsellor. As a person of great expertise and mature judgment, his advice was eagerly sought in India and abroad. He served with distinction as Ambassador to the US and Governor of Jammu and Kashmir. He was at the time of his death, a member of the Rajya Sabha.

As Chairman of the Economic Administration Reforms Commission, he was responsible for changing the direction of economic policy towards controlled deregulation as a preliminary step towards full liberalisation. Furthermore, as Chairman of the Indirect Taxation Enquiry Committee, he made numerous valuable and enduring contributions to the improvement of India's fiscal system. He effectively pleaded the cause of India and other developing countries in many international fora and was a highly respected member of the Brandt Commission. His expertise in the economic field was recognised not only nationally, but also internationally. He was the first Indian Chairman of GATT in 1957-58. He was also Chairman of the UN Group of Eminent Persons on Transnational Corporations, and a member of Interim Coordinate Committee of the International Commodity Agreement. He argued for a new economic order in which the developing countries would have a more equitable share and laid emphasis on strengthening the international institutions which in his view could contribute immensely to the betterment of developing countries.

Jha authored several books—mention may be made of *Economic Development: Ends and Means, Shortages and High Prices: The Way Out, Economic Strategy for the Eighties—Priorities for the Seventh Plan, The North-South Debate, Growth, Inflation and Other Issues, India's Economic Development: A Critique*, and lastly, *Mr. Redtape*, a satirical comment on bureaucratic procedures.

IX.   Governor Shri B.N. Adarkar
(04-05-1970 to 15-06-1970)

There are five 'Stop-Gap' Governors of RBI—Shri K.G. Ambegaonkar, Shri B.N. Adarkar, Shri N.C. Sengupta, Shri M. Narasimham and Shri Amitabh Ghosh.

B.N. Adarkar was the 9th Governor from 1 May 1970 to 15 June 1970. His term was the second shortest—42 days—after that of Amitabh Ghosh who had served for only 20 days. B.N. Adarkar held the post of Governor during the interregnum, until S. Jagannathan could take over as Governor.

Unlike his predecessors who were from the ICS, Adarkar was an economist and had served in the office of Economic Adviser of the GoI. He also held important positions in the Ministry of Commerce

& Industry, prior to his appointment as the Deputy Governor of the Bank. He also served as India's Executive Director at the IMF for about four years, He played an active role in the establishment of the National Institute of Bank Management. He was the Deputy Governor of the RBI before becoming interim Governor. In March 1923, before Indian independence, he was appointed by the GoI to create a Health Insurance Scheme for industrial workers. A year later, the report he submitted became the basis for the Employment State Insurance (ESI) Act of 1948.

During his tenure, the Indian rupee notes of denominations 2, 5, 10, and 100, commemorating the birth centenary of Mahatma Gandhi, was reissued on 24 August 1970. These notes bear his signature, whereas the earlier issue bears that of L.K. Jha.

X. **Shri S. Jagannathan**
(16-06-1970 to 19-05-1975)

S. Jagannathan, the 10th Governor of the RBI was a member of the ICS. He was Governor from 16 June 1970 to 19 May 1975. He had served the Central government in the Ministries of Finance, Industry and Commerce, Partition Secretariat, the Ministry of Transport and the Railways Ministry where he was the Financial Commissioner. He was also Secretary to the Government, Ministry of Finance for two years and thereafter India's Executive Director at the World Bank— prior to his assuming office as the Governor.

Like his predecessors, Iengar and Bhattacharyya, Jagannathan was a student of science. He was educated at the Presidency College, Madras and started his career as a research scholar at the Indian Institute of Science and later studied at the London School of Economics (LSE).

His tenure of office was characterised by a very active monetary policy in the wake of unprecedented inflation in the country, following the oil shock of the 1970s. The bank rate was taken up from the level of 5 per cent to 9 per cent. There was an exponential expansion of banking offices in pursuance of one of the important objectives of nationalisation; the establishment of Credit Guarantee Corporation of India; the setting up of State Level Bankers' Committees; and facilitation of the shift to a floating rates regime. His tenure marked the setting up of the Credit Planning Cell, introduction of the Basic Statistical Returns to collect banking statistics, and amendment of the Foreign Exchange Regulation Act (FERA) 1947 and its rechristening as FERA 1973.

Indian rupee notes of 20 and 50 denominations were introduced, and these bore his signature.

He relinquished office of the Governor just four weeks prior to the completion of his five-year term in order to take up the post of the Indian Executive Director at the IMF.

XI.   Governor Shri N.C. Sen Gupta
(19-05-1975 to 19-08-1975)

N.C. Sen Gupta was the 11th Governor of the RBI from 19 May 1975 to 19 August 1975.

According to *RBI History-Volume III*:

> Sen Gupta's tenure of three months was uneventful. By the time he took over, the slack season policy for 1975 had already been announced. His Governorship, as a result, was conspicuous by the absence of any policy initiative. The only reason he had been appointed was that the Prime Minister and the Finance Minister could not agree on who should succeed S. Jagannathan.

He was the interim Governor, until K.R. Puri took office. Prior to that, he was the Secretary to the Department of Banking of the Ministry of Finance. Even though his tenure was short, his signature appears on the Indian rupee note of 1,000 denomination. This is the only note that bears his signature.

XII. Governor Shri K.R. Puri
(20-08-1975 to 02-05-1977)

K.R. Puri was the 12th Governor of the Reserve Bank of India from 20 August 1975 to 21 May 1977. According to *RBI History-Volume III*:

> ..K.R. Puri was neither Secretary in the Finance Ministry nor an expert on macro-economics. In fact he came from the Insurance sector. There was a difference of opinion between Prime Minister Indira Gandhi and the Finance Minister C. Subramaniam over his appointment. While the Finance Minister had considered economists like I.G. Patel, Narayan Prasad, S.R. Sen and M.G. Kaul as possible names for the post of Governor, the Prime Minister proposed the name of K.R. Puri, Chairman, Life Insurance Corporation of India.

The Finance Minister had to bow before the Prime Minister's wishes.

Dr Krishnaswamy who was a Deputy Governor at that time has narrated in his delectable memoirs, *Windows of Opportunity* about ways in which, during the Emergency, the Prime Minister's Office (PMO) used the office of the Governor of RBI. According to him:

> The intrusion of politics into banking affairs became wider after the declaration of the Emergency. It soon became clear in the RBI that with the appointment of Puri as Governor and Luther as his adviser, financial institutions had become an extension of the PMO, or even worse, of her close advisers....Puri had all along been in the life insurance business and hardly understood central banking.

Dr Krishnaswamy, as Deputy Governor of RBI, refused to provide loan to Maruti, floated by Sanjay Gandhi, son of the then Prime Minister Indira Gandhi. However, the PMO instructed Puri to approve it, which he did without informing Krishnaswamy. Krishnaswamy wanted to be relieved of the responsibility for such loans and Puri assured him that it would not happen again. It did not. However, Sanjay Gandhi and his cronies then started borrowing freely from virtually every bank in Delhi.

M. Narasimham, who was the then Banking Secretary and succeeded

Puri as Governor, has in his book, *From Reserve Bank to the Finance Ministry and Beyond* graphically recounted the story behind K.R. Puri's resignation.

> When H.M. Patel took over as Finance Minister, almost the first thing that he told me was that the RBI Governor K.R. Puri had to go. He said this was also the Prime Minister's express instructions. Puri was persona non grata with the Prime Minister and the Finance Minister as he was reputed to have had close links with what used to be called the extra-constitutional authority during the Emergency and his appointment as governor was regarded as a pure political decision and not based on merit......I would persuade Puri to send in his resignation....As we neared the end of April. I telephoned Puri to come over to Delhi with his resignation letter, which he did and.. I took the letter across to Patel.

During K.R. Puri's tenure, regional rural banks were set up; the Asian Clearing Union commenced operations; the twenty point economic programme was announced and operationalised, and a new money supply series was introduced. His signature appears on one of the last Indian rupee notes of 1,000 denomination. These notes were demonetised in 1978, and were re-introduced after a period of 22 years in 2000.

XIII. Shri M. Narasimham
(02-05-1977 to 30-11-1977)

Maidavolu Narasimham was the 13th Governor of the RBI from 2 May 1977 to 30 November 1977. He was the first and so far the only Governor who had worked earlier in the RBI, having joined the Bank as a Research Officer in the Department of Research and Statistics. He later joined the Government where he served as Additional Secretary, Department of Economic Affairs in 1972. In 1976, he was Secretary, Banking, from where he rose to become RBI Governor.

He wrote in his memoirs, "My tenure in the Reserve Bank was rather uneventful...My attitude was to carry on and, to use a maritime expression, to see the ship's steady as she goes."

After his short term of seven months as RBI Governor, he served as India's Executive Director at the World Bank and later at the IMF— after which he served as Secretary in the Ministry of Finance. He was Chairperson of the Committee on the Financial System, 1991 and the Committee of Banking Sector Reforms, 1998.

According to ex-Governor Venkitaramanan

> During his time in the RBI, Narasimham contributed a number of ideas, some of which later blossomed into full institutions. He played a role in the evolution of the IDBI. In a paper produced at Governor Rama Rau's instance on the utilisation of the so-called Cooley funds generated as a result of PL-480 operation, he suggested to the Governor that these funds might be utilised to set up a refinancing agency, which led to the setting up of the Refinancing Corporation, whose functions subsequently got merged with the Industrial Development Bank of India.

The National Credit Council was another idea that Narasimham initiated and which has disappeared over time. One of his contributions during his period as Additional Secretary, Finance, which evolved from a discussion with Mr C. Subramaniam, was the suggestion to set up regional rural banks. We owe to Narasimham for the introduction of a trade-weighted basket of currencies in order to determine the exchange rate. This scheme, which held sway until the reforms of 1992, marked a step in the move of the country from exchange rate pegged to the sterling to its current state of being determined by the market.

It may be recalled that as Chairman of the two Committees on the financial system, he recommended dismantling of the priority credit system—a system that he himself had helped to introduce. Special interest was attached to the competent manner in which he piloted the intricate negotiations with the IMF on the 1981 loan request made by the Government. Mr Narasimham's reminiscences give a graphic recital of the various negotiations and circumstances that led to the Government's request, following the oil price increases of the late 1970s and the pressure on the balance of payments.

Subsequent to his voluntary retirement from government service and his work as Principal of the Administrative Staff College of India, Hyderabad, Mr Narasimham served for a term in Asian Development Bank (ADB), Manila, where he was Vice-President.

RBI History-Volume III quotes approvingly what the President of the World Bank, Robert McNamara had to say of Narasimham's contribution to the World Bank Board:

> Your dedication, your consistently thoughtful and informed views, your careful judgment, your breadth of vision and your dogged hard work have all combined to set a standard of service on the Board that deserves the gratitude, not only of India and your other constituencies but of the entire development community itself.

He was awarded Padma Vibhushan by the GoI in 2000. His books are *World Economic Environment and Prospects for India* and *Economic Reforms, Development and Finance*. His memoirs are entitled, *From Reserve Bank to Finance Ministry and Beyond*.

XIV. Dr I.G. Patel
(01-12-1977 to 15-09-1982)

Indraprasad Gordhanbhai Patel was the 14th Governor of the RBI from 1 December 1977 to 15 September 1982. He was an eminent economist and distinguished administrator. He was Secretary in the Ministry of Finance. He became the Deputy Administrator of the United Nations Development Programme (UNDP). Later, he was appointed as the Governor of the RBI. His tenure witnessed the 'Gold Auctions' conducted by the Bank on the behalf of GoI. During his tenure, six more private sector banks were nationalised, targets for priority sector lending were introduced, the Deposit Insurance and Credit Guarantee Corporations were merged, and a Departmental reorganisation was undertaken in the Bank. He played an active role in availing of the IMF's Extended Fund Facility in 1981 due to balance of payments difficulties. This represented the largest arrangement made in IMF's history at the time.

The Indian rupee notes of 1,000, 5,000 and 10,000 denominations were demonetised during his tenure. However, the 1,000 notes had to be reintroduced later. He featured on a special commemorative 1,000 rupee note.

In his book, *Glimpses of Indian Economic Policy*, Patel wrote of RBI: "..Nothing approaching a systematic and coherent set of policies was pursued.... routine duties were performed and there was much posturing, but little planning or purpose." There was severe labour problem during his tenure including a strike.

After retiring from the RBI, he became the Director of the Indian Institute of Management, Ahmedabad (IIM-A) in 1982, and helped launch the IIM-A on a trajectory to become the best management school in India.

"There is a vacant chair at every cabinet meeting of Jawaharlal Nehru. It is reserved for the ghost of Prof Harold Laski", according to an article by Ramachandra Guha, eminent historian. This famous statement brings out clearly the paramount influence on Indian administration of the LSE. Dr I.G. Patel was the first professional economist at the helm of the LSE. Patel's brilliant captaincy of LSE led to a coveted KBE—Knighthood from the British Queen. He had a wide, all-enveloping grasp, sharpness of intellect, breadth and sweep of understanding, and freshness and clarity of views—all these left his audiences spellbound. He was an economist of international repute, a brilliant scholar who brought excellence to whatever he touched, a distinguished teacher, and a sensitive administrator. Patel's versatile intellectual personality enabled him to roam with equal ease in his writings and economic adviser's role on the national as well as the international scene, which were all inextricably linked with his personal life. Patel made a successful transition from an academic economist to an economic administrator. He was that rare kind of economist who can simultaneously think and act. His grip over economic theory and the complex facts of economic life was highly commendable.

He was the Director of the LSE from 1984 to 1990. According to Lord Meghnad Desai:

> I.G. Patel was a distinguished architect of economic policymaking in his capacity as an Indian and an international civil servant. He was the first person of South Asian origin to head a higher education institute in the UK and was well known for his formidable intellectual powers in the select company of central bankers and economic statesmen such as the 'Committee of the Thirty' set up by the former German chancellor Helmut Schmidt...His distinguished directorship saw the school's reputation excel to being that of the finest economics school in the world, especially enhancing LSE in India, and Asia as a whole. He was made an honorary fellow of the School in 1990. Later, he taught at the Maharaja Sayajirao University of Baroda.

In 1991, Patel was requested by the then Prime Minister, Narasimha Rao to assume the responsibility of the Finance Minister of India, but he declined this offer. He was bestowed the Padma Vibhushan award in 1991 for his contribution to the field of economic science.

The story of Patel's life charts the rise of his community in India's life. He surprised everyone by coming first in the Matriculation examination and established a record score that was never beaten. He then topped in his Bachelor of Arts (BA) at the University of Bombay and went on to King's College, Cambridge, with a scholarship from the Gaekwars of Baroda. His tutor, Sir Austin Robinson regarded him as his best tutee over his entire tenure as Fellow of King's. Patel returned to India and joined Baroda College as Professor of Economics and Principal in 1949, but was taken away the following year to join the Research Department of the IMF by Edward Bernstein, who became his mentor. After five years there, Patel came back to Delhi as Economic Adviser to the Ministry of Finance in 1954 and spent the next 18 years in one or other top capacity under the GoI.

In 1972, he became the Deputy Administrator of the UNDP for five years, only returning to take up the position of the Governor of the RBI. It was during this period marked by turbulence in the foreign exchange markets that Patel's formidable intellectual powers came into use during sessions of the Bank for International Settlements.

He returned to his native town of Vadodara, but continued his hectic schedule of advising governments and institutions. He wrote succinct accounts of his experience as an economic policymaker in *Glimpses of Indian Economic Policy: An Insider's View*; and of the LSE in *An Encounter with Higher Education: My Years at LSE*. His posthumous book, edited by Dr Y.V. Reddy and Dr Deena Khatkhate, *On Economics* was released by Governor Subbarao.

Patel was present during the creation of the post-war policy infrastructure for economic development in Washington and in Delhi. He was involved in the Indian Second Five Year Plan in 1956 as well as the later two Plans; he participated in successful developing of the reputation of the UNDP; he searched for solutions to the international currency crises in the aftermath of breakdown of the Bretton Woods System; and he consolidated the reputation of the RBI as an architect of monetary stability.

Even after retirement, he was closely associated as Chairman of the Committee for writing of history of the RBI; as a Member of the Board of Management of the Indira Gandhi Institute of Development Research; and as Chairman of the Committee for Licensing of New Private Sector Banks.

XV.   Dr Manmohan Singh
       (16-09-1982 to 14-01-1985)

Dr Manmohan Singh was the 15th Governor of the Reserve Bank from 16 September 1982 to 14 January 1985. He studied at the Universities of Punjab, Cambridge and Oxford. In 1960, he went to the Oxford University for the DPhil. His 1962 doctoral thesis under supervision of Prof I.M.D. Little was titled "India's Export Performance, 1951–1960: Export Prospects and Policy Implications", and later served as the basis for his book *India's Export Trends and Prospects for Self-Sustained Growth*.

After a brief spell of teaching, Dr Manmohan Singh worked with the United Nations Conference on Trade and Development (UNCTAD) Secretariat in several capacities and also taught at the Delhi School of Economics. He held the positions of Economic Adviser, Ministry of Trade, Chief Economic Adviser, Ministry of Finance and Secretary to GoI, Ministry of Finance. Prior to his appointment as the Governor, he was Member, Secretary of the Planning Commission. Following his tenure at the Planning Commission, he was Secretary General of the South Commission, an independent economic policy think tank headquartered in Geneva, Switzerland from 1987 to November 1990. Singh returned to India from Geneva and held the post as the Adviser to Prime Minister of India on economic affairs during the tenure of V.P. Singh. In March 1991, he became Chairman of the Union Public Services Commission and subsequently the Chairman of UGC.

During his tenure as Governor, comprehensive legal reforms were carried out related to the banking sector; a new chapter was introduced in the Reserve Bank of India Act; and the Urban Banks Department was set up.

After his tenure in the Bank, he served in various capacities before being appointed Finance Minister. His term as Finance Minister marked a paradigm shift in India's economic policy with the launching of path-breaking economic reforms that embraced delicensing of the industrial sector, liberalisation of trade and shift to market-based exchange rate regime. He was the Prime Minister of India since 2004.

The period 2004-2008 is marked by the Indian economy recording the fastest economic growth with stability.

Of his two terms as Prime Minister, it has been averred that there was a precipitous fall from heights of glory to depths of despair, Manmohan Singh struggling to keep his head above the mire of scandals !

XVI. Shri Amitabh Ghosh
  (15-01-1985 to 04-02-1985)

Shri Amitabh Ghosh was the 16th Governor of the RBI. He served for 20 days from 15 January to 4 February 1985. His term was the shortest ever served by any RBI Governor. He held the post until Shri Malhotra could take over.

Shri Ghosh was the Deputy Governor since 1982. Prior to this, he was Chairman of the Allahabad Bank. He was also a Director of the IDBI Bank and was present on the governing body of the National Institute of Bank Management.

XVII. Shri R.N. Malhotra
  (04-02-1985 to 22-12-1990)

Shri R.N. Malhotra was the 17th Governor of the RBI, serving from 4 February 1985 to 22 December 1990. He had served as Secretary, Finance, and as India's Executive Director of the IMF before his appointment as Governor of the RBI.

Shri R.N. Malhotra was also an Officer of the Indian Administrative Service (IAS) and had served as Secretary, Finance, before taking over as Governor of the RBI. His appointment came immediately following the landmark recommendations of the Chakravarty Committee on the monetary system. During his tenure, efforts were made to widen the money markets and new instruments were introduced. Shri Malhotra was instrumental in setting up the Indira Gandhi Institute of Development and Research in 1987. The Discount and Finance House of India as well as the National Housing Bank was set up in 1988. In the field of rural finance, the Service Area Approach was introduced in order to catalyse credit flow to rural India through commercial banks.

During his tenure, the 500-rupee note was introduced. He also signed the new 50-rupee note in 1986.

The latest *RBI History-Volume IV* quotes with approval the memorandum to the Central Board of Directors, dated 21 January 1991.

> As Governor of the Reserve Bank of India, he (Shri Malhotra) strove to ensure that the Bank contributed effectively towards achieving the national goal of growth with stability, particularly through its monetary and credit policies and that the country's financial system remained sound. He provided the impetus for a more flexible, transparent and competitive financial system and more significant contributions in ensuring that the banking system adopted prudential norms and took particular interest in ensuring improved housekeeping by banks.

XVIII. Shri S. Venkitaramanan
(22-12-1990 to 21-12-1992)

Shri S. Venkitaramanan, a distinguished member of the IAS, had served as a policymaker in the Central and State Governments. He was Financial Secretary to the GoI from February 1985 to March 1989. Thereafter, he served as Adviser to the Prime Minister and then to the Government of Karnataka for a short time, prior to his appointment as the 18th Governor in December 1990.

Shri Venkitaramanan had a relatively short stint at the RBI (22 December 1990 to 21 December 1992). Major economic reforms were initiated during his regime. The country faced difficulties related to the external sector and his adroit management saw the country tide over the balance of payments crisis. His term also saw India adopt the IMF's stabilisation programme where the rupee underwent a devaluation, and also the launch of the programme of economic reforms. His energies towards the latter part of his tenure were diverted by a major financial scam involving irregularities in Securities Transactions, which also embroiled the National Housing Bank, a subsidiary of the RBI.

Shri Venkitaramanan holds a Master's degree in Physics from University College, Trivandrum and also a Master's Degree in Industrial Administration from Carnegie Mellon University, Pittsburg, US. He has published a number of books on Indian economy.

After serving as Governor of the RBI, he has been writing regularly in the financial dailies.

XIX. Dr C. Rangarajan
(22-12-1992 to 21-12-1997)

Dr Rangarajan was Member of the Planning Commission before taking over as the 19th Governor of the RBI in December 1992. Earlier, he had worked as a Deputy Governor, moving on from academia. He was instrumental in making some historic changes to monetary policy management. His tenure as Governor saw unprecedented Central Bank activism to put in place a comprehensive set of measures in order to strengthen and improve competitive efficiency of the financial sector. New institutions and instruments were introduced and changes in exchange rate management culminated in the establishment of a unified exchange rate. The latest volume of *RBI History* declares, "Dr Rangarajan pushed forward monetary and financial sector reforms and ended the four-decades practice of automatic monetization of the fiscal deficit through active co-ordination with the Government." A historic memorandum was signed between the Bank and the Government whereby a cap was put on the automatic finance done by the former to the latter in the form of ad hoc treasury bills, which gave RBI greater autonomy in the conduct of monetary policy.

Dr Rangarajan graduated from Loyola College of the University of Madras in the commerce stream. He later received his PhD in economics from the University of Pennsylvania in 1964. He taught at several institutions including the University of Pennsylvania and the IIM-A. He was a well-known teacher of economics at IIM-A for the postgraduate and the doctoral courses. His textbook on macroeconomics was used in business management schools. He was awarded the title of Honorary Fellow of IIM-A in 1997.

He served as a Deputy Governor of the RBI from 1982 to 1991, after which he served as Governor of the RBI between 22 December 1992 and 21 December 1997. He also served as the Governor of Andhra Pradesh from 1997 to 2003. After demitting that office, he took charge as the Chairman of the Twelfth Finance Commission. Post-2005, he was the Chairman of the Prime Minister's Economic Advisory Council. In August 2008, he resigned from this position and was nominated as a member of the Rajya Sabha. He resigned from the Rajya Sabha in August 2009 and was re-appointed the Chairman of the Prime Minister's Economic Advisory Council.

In 2002, he was accorded the nation's second highest civilian honour, Padma Vibhushan.

He is the author of a large number of books, such as *India's Monetary Policy, Financial Stability and Other Essays*.

XX.   Dr Bimal Jalan
(22-11-1997 to 06-09-2003)

Dr Bimal Jalan had held several important positions before taking over as the 20th Governor of the RBI. These included Chief Economic Adviser to the GoI, Banking Secretary, Finance Secretary, Member-Secretary of the Planning Commission and Chairman of the Prime

Minister's Economic Advisory Council. He also represented India on executive boards of the IMF and World Bank. As Finance Secretary, he was also on the Central Board of Directors of RBI. Jalan was President of the governing body of National Council of Applied Economics Research (NCAER), India's first independent economic policy institute established in 1956.

As Governor, he effectively dealt with the fall out of the Southeast Asian crisis and ensured consolidation of the gains of liberalisation and economic reforms. The monetary policy process was demystified and central bank communications displayed a shift towards transparency. This period has seen a slew of measures to strengthen the banking sector, establish new institutions and introduce new instruments. It has been characterised by strengthening of the balance of payments and forex position, low inflation and soft interest rates. The Foreign Exchange Regulation Act, 1973, was replaced by the Foreign Exchange Management Act, 1999, marking a paradigm shift in the exchange rate management mechanism. During his tenure, the Indian rupee note of 1,000 denomination was introduced.

He was nominated as a Rajya Sabha member on 27 August 2003 and relinquished office as the RBI Governor on 6 September 2003.

Bimal Jalan who was born on 17 August 1941 graduated from Presidency College, Calcutta and later attended Oxford and Cambridge. He has authored many books, such as *The Future of India, India's Politics: A View from the Backbench, The Future Of India: Politics, Economics, And Governance, The Indian Economy: Problems And Prospects, India's Economic Policy, Emerging India: Economics, Politics and Reforms* and *India's Economic Crisis: The Way Ahead*. He was Chairman of the Advisory Committee and had brought out the fourth volume of *RBI History*.

Presently, Dr Jalan is Chairman of the prestigious Centre for Development Studies, Trivandrum, an advanced Institute of economic research founded by Dr K.N. Raj, one of the foremost Indian economists. Dr Jalan is also Chairman of the RBI committee to make recommendations for new Bank Licences.

XXI. Dr Y.V. Reddy
   (06-09-2003 to 05-09-2008)

Dr Yaga Venugopal Reddy, the 21st Governor, is a member of the IAS. He has spent most of his career in the areas of finance and planning. He served as Secretary (Banking) in Ministry of Finance, Additional Secretary, Ministry of Commerce, Joint Secretary in Ministry of Finance in GoI, Principal Secretary, Government of Andhra Pradesh and had a six-year tenure as Deputy Governor of the RBI. Prior to his appointment as the Governor, Dr Reddy was India's Executive Director on the Board of IMF

A 2008 article in the *New York Times* has credited the tough lending standards that he had imposed on the Indian banks as RBI Governor for the purpose of saving the entire Indian banking system from the sub-prime and liquidity crisis of 2008. During his tenure at the RBI, the Indian economy achieved the highest growth rate in three consecutive years. He had to deal with a sharp increase in capital inflows and overheating of the economy towards the end of his tenure. Monetary operations were strengthened with the introduction of Market Stabilisation Scheme bonds. Banking services for the common man was Dr Reddy's core concern, and he took a number of steps to safeguard financial stability. He shielded the Indian economy from the worst impact of the global financial crisis. In one of his interviews, Joseph E. Stiglitz, Professor of Economics at Columbia University and Nobel Laureate, had said, "If America had a central bank chief like Y.V. Reddy, the US economy would not have been in such a mess".

Dr Reddy is a Master of Arts in economics from Madras University and a PhD from Osmania University. He also holds a Diploma in Economic Planning from the Institute of Social Studies, Netherlands. On 17 July 2008, Reddy was made an Honorary Fellow of the LSE. He is the author of several books—*India and the Global Financial Crisis: Managing Money and Finance, Global Crisis, Recession and Uneven Recovery* and *Economic Policies and India's Reform Agenda: New Thinking.* Dr Reddy is currently Professor Emeritus, University of Hyderabad. He is also Honorary Fellow of the London School of Economics and

Political Science. He is the Chairman of the 14th Finance Commission, since 3 January 2013.

Dr Reddy was honoured with the Padma Vibhushan Award in 2010.

XXII. Dr D. Subbarao
(05-09-2008 to 04-09-2013)

Dr D. Subbarao, an officer of the IAS, assumed office as the 22nd Governor of the RBI on 5 September 2008 at the height of the global financial crisis. Prior to his appointment, Dr Subbarao was the Finance Secretary in the Ministry of Finance, GoI. In a short span of six months at the RBI, he made sharp adjustments in the interest rates and instituted a host of other conventional and unconventional measures to safeguard the Indian economy from adverse impact of the global financial crisis. He placed emphasis on transparency in monetary policy communication and on financial inclusion.

Dr Subbarao was earlier Secretary to the Prime Minister's Economic Advisory Council (2005-2007), lead economist in the World Bank (1999-2004), Finance Secretary to the Government of Andhra Pradesh (1993-1998) and Joint Secretary in the Department of Economic Affairs, Ministry of Finance, GoI (1988-1993).

He has wide experience in public finance. In the World Bank, he worked on issues of public finance in countries of Africa and East Asia. He managed a flagship study on decentralisation across major countries of East Asia, including China, Indonesia, Vietnam, Philippines and Cambodia. Dr Subbarao was also involved in initiation of fiscal reforms at the state level. Dr Subbarao has written extensively on issues in public finance, decentralisation and political economy of reforms.

Dr Subbarao holds a BSc (Honours) in Physics from the Indian Institute of Technology (IIT) Kharagpur and MSc in Physics from IIT, Kanpur. He also holds a MS degree in Economics from Ohio State

University. He was a Humphrey fellow at Massachusetts Institute of Technology (MIT) during 1982-83. He has a PhD in Economics with thesis on fiscal reforms at the sub-national level. Dr Subbarao was a topper in the All India Civil Service examination for entry into IAS and Indian Foreign Services in 1972. He was one of the first IIT-ians to join the civil service.

However, it was during Subbarao's tenure that the value of Indian rupee tumbled spectacularly, along with USD/INR exchange rate breaching the psychological barrier of 60 for the first time and even hitting a new low of 69.

XXIII. Dr Raghuram Rajan
(From 04-09-2013)

Dr Raghuram Rajan assumed charge as the 23rd Governor of the RBI on 4 September 2013. Prior to this, he was the Chief Economic Adviser, Ministry of Finance, GoI and the Eric J. Gleacher Distinguished Service Professor of Finance at the University of Chicago's Booth School. Between 2003 and 2006, Dr Rajan was the Chief Economist and Director of Research at the IMF.

Dr Rajan's research interests are related to banking, corporate finance and economic development, especially the role play by finance. He has co-authored *Saving Capitalism from the Capitalists* with Luigi Zingales in 2003. He then wrote *Fault Lines: How Hidden Fractures Still Threaten the World Economy*, for which he was awarded the Financial Times-Goldman Sachs prize for the best business book in 2010.

Dr Rajan is a member of the Group of Thirty. He was the President of the American Finance Association (AFA) in 2011 and is a member of the American Academy of Arts and Sciences. In January 2003, the AFA awarded Dr Rajan the inaugural Fischer Black Prize for the best finance researcher under the age of 40. The other awards that he has received include the Global Indian of the Year Award from the National

Association of Software and Services Companies (NASSCOM) in 2011, the Infosys prize for the Economic Sciences in 2012, and the Center for Financial Studies-Deutsche Bank Prize for financial economics in 2013.

Dr Rajan, who was born on 3 February 1963, is the youngest person to have been appointed RBI Governor after Independence.

PART-III

Anecdotes

When I joined the Reserve Bank of India (RBI) on 4 December 1956, the Governor was Sir Benegal Rama Rau—the second Indian Governor. Forty years later when I retired on 31 October 1996, the Governor was Dr C. Rangarajan, who was the 19th Governor. Thus I had worked under 17 Governors. An item I cherish is my rare collection of all the card calendars issued by RBI from 1956 to 1996. I have ensured that my collection includes the very latest 2014—in all 59 calendars. Another prized possession is the first computerised pay-slip for the month of March 1957. I enjoyed a basic salary of ₹ 110 and drew allowances of ₹ 57, totalling ₹ 167. With a deduction of ₹ 11 towards PF (provident fund), I had the princely take-home pay of ₹ 156.

Before I begin, I want to gladly mention that during the three years after Platinum Jubilee of RBI, I have published my reviews of 44 books by either RBI Executives or on RBI. The books reviewed are the latest works of Drs. Reddy, Rangarajan, Rakesh Mohan, V.V. Bhatt, D.R. Khatkhate, Sarvashri A.G. Chandavarkar, V.G. Pendharkar and a book of tribute to S.L.N. Simha. I got appreciative letters for my reviews from Governor Subbarao, Drs Reddy, Rangarajan, Rakesh Mohan and Narayana Murthy. The book, *Governors Speak* was sent to me by Governor Subbarao.

In this trip down memory lane, I shall recount some historical events of these four decades, to some of which I am privy and some I learnt from reliable seniors. My first set of anecdotes relate to Governors; my second set with the Economic Department; and the last two to dear friends.

•

I had the privilege of being the liason officer of Governor Shri R.N. Malhotra, when he came for the Central Board meeting in Trivandrum. He desired to visit the ancestral house of his wife. I was assigned the task of taking him there. He was accorded status of a State Governor and resided in the Raj Bhavan. I took him from there at 8 am. We were in an Ambassador car with a police jeep ahead of us blaring a siren. The van behind us carried half a dozen policemen. We reached Anna Malhotra's house; the Governor spent some time talking (through me) to some old relatives. As we were about to depart, Governor's brother-in-law barged in and asked me to request the Governor to get a job for his son. I duly transmitted the request. Malhotra frowned and asked me to tell him to go to hell. What I told him in Malayalam was: "There are several worlds for your son." The Governor appeared happy at my long sentence and we drove back to Raj Bhavan.

•

This story relates to the visit, in February 1958, to RBI of the Managing Director of the International Monetary Fund (IMF)—the noted Swedish banker, Per Jacobsson. When Jacobsson was leaving for Delhi, Governor H.V.R. Iengar and Shri V.G. Pendharkar went to the airport to see him off. Jacobsson was tall and quite a hefty person. As he walked towards the plane, an Air-India Boeing 707, Governor Iengar asked Pendharkar how much he thought Jacobsson weighed. Pendharkar guesstimated about 175 pounds. Iengar said, "No, he was much more than that. And just when Jacobsson entered the plane, one of its tyres blew, as if to protest to the heavy weight thrust upon it without warning. Iengar said, "My God! Look what has happened. Even the plane has sunk under his weight!"

Janakiraman's Day One in RBI

He was denied admission by the *durwan*. He was dressed in a flat white *dhoti*, white full shirt, and a black alpaca coat (generally worn by lawyers). He had a luxuriant tuft in which flowers were tucked in. He was in simple chappals and carried an old black box. No doubt the *durwan* barred his entry as he thought he was a salesman. When he told that he had come from Madras for an interview for Officer's post in RBI, the *durwan* allowed him. This was the maiden entry of R. Janakiraman (RJ) to the majestic old main building. On the interview board were three Deputy Governors, Venkatappiah, Sundaresan and Ramnath. All were in western attire—one sporting even a bow tie. They were amused to see this candidate. However, they were impressed when they learnt that he held a postgraduate degree in Geography and displayed a score of gold medals he had amassed during his academic career. The Board asked him a number of questions which he answered with ease. Then one of the Deputy Governors (DGs) told him about the dress code for RBI: "You will have to remove your *shikha* or tuft and have a crop: Will you do it?" "Certainly not," answered the candidate. "Why?" asked an aghast DG. "Since you have not offered me a firm job, I am apt to lose my favourite tuft and also not get the job." They had a hearty laugh and asked him to join the RBI then and there. RJ rose to the level of DG. He recounted this story at his send off. You can read, elsewhere in this book, my speech at the send-off function.

•

I belong to the original Avatara of the present MPD—namely the Credit Planning Cell during the halcyon days of the redoubtable Shri A. Raman. I was an SO—Staff Officer, and with me was Usha Thorat—a JO—Junior Officer. Over the years, I have moved out of the Bank and Usha Thorat has moved up to become a DG. And happily Pranab Mukherjee has announced that the next RBI Governor will be a woman. I do wish that one of my two erstwhile colleagues—Usha Thorat and Shyamala Gopinath—becomes Governor. I have worked in the Department of Banking Operations and Development (DBOD) with the latter. I was wondering how we will address her! Governess Shyamala Gopinath/Usha Thorat or simply Madam Governor. I do recall with joy that fairly regularly, the Governor Shri S. Jagannathan would walk into our Credit Planning Cell (CPC) and sit down on equal terms with us.

Now I turn to my life in the Economic Department.

The year is 1956—over half a century ago. I joined the RBI and was posted to the DRS—the Department of Research and Statistics— the ancestor of today's Department of Economic Analysis and Policy (DEAP)—affectionately called the Department of Rest and Sleep! It comprised a number of divisions and I got posted to the Administration Division and in-charge of the Leave Desk. One morning a peon came running to me and said, "Narasimham Sab Bulatha Hai." I went to his cabin, knocked and then entered. He was barely visible behind a huge desk full of papers, file boards and a pile of books. I greeted him and introduced myself. He smiled a boyish smile and asked, "Mr Ramachandran, I wonder whether you can tell me the casual leave to my credit." Without batting an eyelid, I shot back, "You need not wonder! If you give me a couple of minutes I shall enlighten you." Narasimham laughed loudly and said, "Young man, it is just a phrase!" That was my first lesson in English from the then Deputy Director, M. Narasimham who went on to become RBI's Secretary and Governor. He asked me to read the *London Economist* and the *Economic and Political Weekly* (EPW)—both of which I religiously read even today.

•

I moved from Administration to the Division of Monetary Research headed by Shri P.V. Ranganathan. He was always immaculately attired in white trousers and shirt and a colourful tie and coat. He was known for his temper and tantrums. Stories about him are legion, but I shall restrict myself to one. He had joined the Bank as a Research Superintendent. Fresh from Madras, understandably of Hindi and Marathi he was innocent. One evening as closing time approached, he decided to sit for some time to clear some urgent work and instructed his peon not to keep his papers in the cupboard. That worthy, not having followed his instruction in English began keeping his papers in the cupboard. Ranganathan got wild and shouted at him: "You fool. I told you not to keep my papers in!" No sooner was this sentence uttered than was heard the loud sound of a hand slapping a face. The peon moved out of the hall, en route cut his face with a blade and complained to Administration that he was beaten by Ranganathan, which left him bleeding. After first aid, the Administrative Officer conducted an enquiry and learnt from whoever was present that only the sound of a slap was heard, but as to who slapped whom they had no idea. The peon got the benefit of doubt and Ranganathan was warned to be more careful and the case was closed!

•

There was another Director who was famous for his bouts of anger and torrential tirade. He summoned his Deputy Director at 12.30 pm and instructed him to prepare a note on revising the Bank Rate. And he added: "The note must be on my desk by 2 pm"—quite a forbidding task. But the Deputy was up for any emergency, worked hard and followed his boss's instruction. The Director returned at 2 pm and was happy to see a file board with a note. He called his Deputy, asked him to sit down and began reading loudly the note. "Good. Very good. Well argued," he said. As he reached the last page, he found another note of similar dimension lurking below. "What is this?" he bellowed. The Deputy answered calmly, "Sir, you had not instructed me whether there should be a rise in Bank rate or a fall. The second note argues for a fall of one per cent!"

•

One of the highly respected officials of the Economic Department was Dr T.K. Velayudham (TKV), son of a humble station master in Andhra Pradesh (AP). TKV held the Chair in Monetary Economics established by RBI in the Bombay University. When he was my Deputy Director, he took part in worldwide essay competition conducted by *The Banker* magazine, London. He bagged the first prize. The next year also he received the first prize. When the magazine announced a competition for the third year in succession, they wrote a letter to him requesting him not to participate and leave the prize for others. He retired as Principal of Bankers' Training College (BTC).

•

We had an Economic Assistant who always wore suits and matching ties. His Officer was the emblem of simplicity—trouser and half bush-shirt. Once our Director wanted something immediately about cement prices and had contacted Nani Palkhiwala. The latter had instructed him to send his representatives. So the Officer and Assistant went to the Office of ACC. They were taken to the chamber of Palkhiwala who gave the details required. The Officer had brought a pad and pencil in which he was noting certain points. Palkhiwala noticed this and told the be-suited Assistant, "If you want anything more I shall give you happily. Only send your stenographer. You need not waste your valuable time." The duo were appropriately shocked, especially the Officer.

•

To come down from high executive levels, I had two close friends— Shri Shirali and Shri Gopalan. I knew of Shirali's profound knowledge of Marxism and Marxist literature. Among people he admired were S.A. Dange, Asok Mitra and Ranadive. The Indian Institute of Marxist Theory and Practice has brought out a book and dedicated it to Shri D.U. Shirali. The book is entitled *Whither Indian Republic?*

Shirali was the subject of many stories in the Department we worked in—most of them comical—the recounting of which he himself would enjoy. He would get angry at a lightning speed and go at the throat of his opponent but with equal speed he would reconcile and the two would be found with hands around each other's shoulders. I had taken Shirali and got stitched for him a new pair of trousers from Joe-

Martyn, the best tailor in Fort. The next day, it was the anniversary of his father. Shirali had taken permission to come late to Office. Though the ceremonies began early, it was taking a long time and worried about office, Shirali who was in his *dhoti* in traditional fashion put on the new trousers and ran to work. He found that he could not sit in the train and also movement had become tough! He cursed me for choosing Joe-Martyn. After managing reaching office, he was aghast to learn in the bathroom that he had not removed his dhoti before putting on his new trousers!

•

R.S. Gopalan had a ready wit always. He bubbled with effervescence of vintage champagne and it was unthinkable not to laugh when Gopalan was around. During his last days, he fell inside a moving bus, cracked his hip bone and was compelled to wear a belt always. He told me, "They say, people died with their boots on. In my case they will say, "Gopalan died with his belt on." In a few days, he passed away. He had worked in the Economic Department Library for long years. There were two assistants in that library, Shri Shah and Shri Singh. An associate from the library, who had resigned and gone abroad came on a holiday and visited the library. The first question he asked was, "Are Shah and Singh still in the library?" Gopalan's prompt response was—"Mr Sadhwani, once upon a time Shah and Singh were features of the library. Now they are fixtures."

•

Another good colleague who formed my "Three Musketeers," along with Shri.Shirali and Shri Gopalan was Shri Sethu. He was a brilliant postgraduate in Economics and a lecturer from Kerala; and when he joined the Department of Research and Statistics, he was pleasantly surprised to note that his student Shri V.J. Paul was already employed there. Sethu was an excellent worker and was held in esteem by the bosses. His ambition to become a Junior Officer unfortunately did not materialise and he languished quite a bit. Swarthy and well-built, he sported a flourishing moustache which would have been envied by the Russian dictator, Joseph Stalin! During free hours, Sethu could be seen engrossed in fat murder mystery novels. A book in one hand, he would twirl a side of his luxuriant moustache and the speed of twirling would increase with the tension prevailing in the book. If he had stopped twirling, you can assume that plot of the story is smooth. After sometime, he would start twirling the other side of his moustache. He and I went for a cancer check-up to St. George Hospital, near Victoria Terminus (VT). There, they asked him if he was attracted to tobacco. His pithy answer floored them; almost like Oscar Wilde he declared, "I smoke—I chew—and I sniff." They were appropriately shocked, but he was happily free of any ailment. He was a deeply religious man, steeped in the traditions of Kerala and he would share his Kerala experiences with all colleagues. He was a keen astrologer and would study the horoscopes of worried friends.

•

A Saga of RBI Office Buildings in Bombay

I had joined the RBI 57 years ago—to be precise on 4 December 1956. I was posted to the Administrative Division of the Department of Research and Statistics in the Amar Building on Sir P.M. Road. As I took the lift, I found a framed certificate to the effect—'This Lift is the property of the Maharaja of Wankaner.' I learnt on enquiry that the Maharaja owned the entire building. The second floor was fully occupied by Bombay Telephones—who also had a portion on the ground floor, which presently is housing the Monetary Museum. Soon the ownership was transferred to the RBI, but Bombay Telephones refused to vacate. I learnt reliably that the then Governor Shri B. Rama Rau wrote to the Finance Minister threatening that if the Bombay Telephones did not vacate in a one month's time, then he would tender his resignation. Within a month, the Telephones Department handed over the floor to RBI. That floor is where, for long and even now, the Class III Canteen and the Officers Lounge exist.

A few years later, I bade goodbye to Amar Building and was posted to Colaba. The building was eloquently named Johny Castle—two divisions of the Economic Department were located there. The building was near the Colaba bus station. The building had two entrances. One led to a den of prostitutes. The other led to a den of economists or budding economists! One day the ceiling of ground floor rooms collapsed, fortunately at 9:30 am. Or else, a few would have died. The Staff stood outside demonstrating for one full week—refusing to enter the building. We were asked to sign the muster outside the building and were allowed to leave at 11:15 am. This went on for a full week. The Economic Adviser arrived to see and consequently attempted to pacify us. Next day we were shifted temporarily to the Economic Department in Amar Building. But since there was no place to sit, we could wander. I spent most of the time in the adjoining Asiatic Library. We finally moved to the Sidhwa House in Colaba.

After a stint of Colaba life, I gravitated to the Agricultural Research and Development Centre (ARDC) in Worli.

The Offices were in two buildings—Poonam Chambers and Shriniketan. During office time, the ceiling in Shriniketan had once collapsed. Luckily, the staff could run away.

I have worked here for five long years. A singular advantage was that it was located within three minutes walk from the Lotus Theatre. This theatre screened art films from 12:30 to 2:00 pm. I have seen over 25 Bengali films—especially the great ones of Satyajit Ray—in the Lotus. Slip out of office at 12:27 pm, Watch the film and be back in the seat by 2:03 pm. Not one soul knew. Only constraint was that I could not discuss these films in ARDC!

I hope there is no provision to retrospectively issue memos to retirees for their violations during service. Alas ! Lotus Theatre has been demolished!

While on the subject of Worli, I can also cover the legendary Garment House which is very close to Worli Naka. Why 'legendary', I will explain now. The Agricultural Credit Department was in this Garment. The building was named so because it was owned by the biggest laundry in Bombay—*viz.* Garment Cleaners. Giant cleaning machines thundered in the ground floor. The three upper floors were overwhelmed by the noise, occasionally suffering from mild tremors! Yet, one advantage should not be overlooked!

The Garment Cleaners offered 50 per cent discount to all the RBI staff. Delivery of clothes given at 10 am in the morning were returned by 4 pm without fail. One could witness the unedifying spectacle of RBI staff residing in nearby staff quarters travelling by contract bus, bring in the morning fat bundles of dirty clothes and returning in the evening with neat packets of clean, well-washed and ironed clothes.

They regretted the closure of the laundry!

•

The Bank sent me out of Bombay to our office in Trivandrum where I spent a happy term of nine years. On return to Mumbai, I became DGM in DBOD in the World Trade Centre (WTC). Once DBOD was located in the Arcade, it later acquired four floors in the adjoining skyscraper—WTC. However, a few offices and canteens/lounges continued to operate in the Arcade. An enviable and enjoyable facility of the Arcade was and is the huge circular entrance, which was used by almost everyone for a post-lunch walk so as to digest food and exchange gossip.

•

I shall now cover some of the Offices where I have not worked.

We had the Bombay Regional Office (BRO) of DBOD located in Ashok Mahal, behind Regal Cinema.

In Masjid Bunder, we had the Industrial Finance Department (IFD) in Commercial Manor—a very busy, crowded storage area with goons brandishing knives. Once there was a fire in the adjoining Mirchi Godown and staff were asked to report after three days until the smoke and dust settled down. Employees had to walk through stinking lanes with flowing gutter water and offal. Several representations were of no avail.

Then one day, a RBI Officer was stabbed and left bleeding. He came in his bloodied shirt to the DG. And immediately went to the Bank's Medical Officer (BMO). The very next day that Office was closed.

Some more buildings with RBI Offices collapsed partly too.

One was in Cowasji Patel Street next to BLITZ Office—the Poddar Chambers. This Office had no toilet for the ladies and they therefore had to go the Main Building. Imagine the plight of those whose needs were very urgent!

Another was in Perin Nariman Street. Makani Manzil—a wing of the IFD was housed here. You could see the collapsed portions—rather the remains from Amar Building. Makani Manzil too had no proper toilet facilities! Staff would have to come to Amar Building across the road.

The Economic Department had three floors in the Marshall Building in Ballard Estate. Due to heavy flooding, the Economic Department Library had lost over 5000 valuable books.

The Department of Statistical Analysis & Computer Services (DESACS) located in Novelty Chambers had all windows closed, but not because of air-conditioning! The opposite building was a house of prostitutes. The location was near a red-light area of Bombay.

The Office of the Banking Commission was in Malabar Hill—known as White House—the sprawling bungalow of R.G. Saraiya. Regardless of the fabulous location, the Office did not provide for tea/coffee/food—and for a week, there was no water! Obviously, tiny hotels are unavailable in such an area. The staff went around demonstrating to all Departments, shouting slogans. "White House is a Black House— White House Black House."

City Ice Building, behind the Old Main Building, had two floors where the staff belonging to Division of Publications of Economic Department worked. Once you climbed down the building, you have to turn right into an alley that led up to the French Bank building. This alley bristled with swarthy African sellers of dope, hasish and drugs. Happily no employee of RBI was dragged into the net.

The building had an ice factory where fishes were preserved and an overpowering smell of fish prevailed always.

Deposit Insurance and Credit Guarantee Corporation of India (DICGC) had its Office—in Phatak Wadi—in Picket Road near Metro Cinema. The Staff there were considered blessed for being within two minutes walk from the blessings of the Swayambhu Hanuman. This temple is 155 years old and popular with ministers, bureaucrats, police officers and celebrities.

There were Offices in Khatau Mansion in Cooperage, Engineering Centre at Opera House which housed United Trust of India (UTI) before delinking, Akbarallys Building at Flora Fountain, New India Centre near Regal, Jolly Makers Bhavan and in Eros Building.

I have not included the more popular structures like Amar Building, Mercantile Bank Building, Old Main Building, Central Office Building—the Skyscraper, BKC. Byculla and Belapur.

I shall conclude with a happy nostalgic event. The late Shri V.A. Mahimkar, eminent Trade Unionist and leading light of RBI Co-operative Society, distinctly recalled being taken by his father to watch a circus in the ground where a few years later the RBI Main building was constructed!

Where are the Guns Now ?
This is culled from a book on Bombay:

Many years ago when the foundation of the RBI's new Tower block, adjacent to the GoI Mint, was being laid, a pair of very large guns were found. Since nobody wanted them and they were too heavy to relocate, they were left untouched and the Skyscraper was constructed over them.

My Trivandrum Days

At the age of 46, the Bank dropped a bombshell on me and shattered my peace of mind. "You are promoted and transferred to Trivandrum" was the official's words. I had two school-going kids and this was the month of December! My greatest worry was that—though a Keralite—I could not speak, read and write in Malayalam! In the event I landed in Trivandrum and reported to the Manager, who posted me as the Head of the Urban Banks Department (UBD). The staff members were excellent. I used to get calls from Urban Banks and I would request Nair or Pillai or Menon to tackle these. They did this pleasantly for a week. And then they cried, "Halt" and asked me to learn and master the language. I started listening to Malayalam news, read daily *Mathrubhoomi* and *Manorama*, and they would all talk to me in Malayalam only. I fell in love with Malayalam films. Within a month, I made rapid progress and handled all calls myself and in a couple of months, visited banks in different centres and managed matter fairly well.

The TVM Office is one of the best buildings among all the RBI offices. It is a huge area in Bakery Junction, where the compound had a large number of imposing coconut trees. Most impressive was a Laburnum tree luxuriant with Konna flowers—important for Vishu festival. That one tree met the needs of over 100 members of the Staff.

Trivandrum is one of the most cultured capitals in the country. Of Fine Arts, there was a cornucopia. Kathakali, Mohini Attam, Bharata Natyam, Ottam Thullal and different dance programmes used to happen throughout the year. I was a member of Soorya—an exclusive film society which screened 54 films in a year—all quality films and both Indian and foreign in nature. Carnatic music poured over liberally.

My worry about the education of my daughters vanished in a jiffy. The quality of education was the highest. My daughters did very well and stood first throughout their career.

The Bank provided us with a brand new bungalow in Pattom. Here my wife grew all types of flowers and vegetables. A wall was full of Madrasi pan. She had also set out Kadipatha and Neem plants. These today—30 years later—are luxuriant giant trees. The bungalow was within walking distance from the RBI Office and my children's school. A luxury for a Mumbaikar like me—who walked, travelled by train and boarded a BEST bus!

The highlight of my tenure was taking RBI Governor Shri R.N. Malhotra to his wife's house. I have recounted this elsewhere in the book. Another memorable item is accompanying Deputy Governor Dr Rangarajan to the Centre for Development Studies (CDS) for breakfast with the legendary Dr K.N. Raj. The lunch was with the eminent Economist, Prof Subramaniam. I had also taken Governor Malhotra to the library of CDS.

Being a small Centre, we were invited for celebrations in Raj Bhavan and got introduced to the State Governor.

While I was Head of the UBD for five years, I was also serving as Head of the Issue Department for three years. Being Currency Officer is no bed of roses and I had to bear the slings and arrows of an outrageous environment of the Issue Department.

I recall with happiness the BMO, who was a genial warm-hearted person. What impressed me most was that he owned eight elephants—a family heirloom.

•

Miss I.T. Vaz

I was head of the UBD in Trivandrum in the late 1980s. One day I got a message that Kum I.T. Vaz, the Head of the UBD in Central Office, Bombay, was paying a visit to our Office and I should receive her at the airport and make necessary arrangements. I went the next morning to the Airport with an Ambassador car and was waiting. The Bombay plane landed and a little later passengers started flowing out. I could spot my boss from a distance and waved my arm. Kum Vaz came near the vehicle and after entering she said, "Mr Ramachandran, I was wondering whether you would be able to recognise me—since we have never met!" I said with a smile, "You are unforgettable, Madam!" Kum Vaz blushed and was astonished to hear this. She asked promptly, "How?" Coolly, I replied, "Madam, because of you, I walked in the hot sun from RBI Main Building to the Governor's residence at Carmichael Road—eight miles away. Because of you, I lost one day's wage. Because of you, my increment is postponed by one day!" She exploded into laughter and said, "This is the first time someone has told this to my face. All utter it behind my back. I am sure we will get along well!" She made three more trips to Trivandrum. There was an Association-sponsored agitation against her promotion.

The Humble Pie

Towards the 19th century, the pie was the smallest minted coin in India. It constituted one third of a pice and was officially termed one twelfth of an anna. Three pies made a pice; 4 pice made an anna and 16 annas made a rupee. One rupee, thus, consisted of 192 pies. (No wonder arithmetic daunted the faint-hearted then!!)

In the wake of the Second World War, India witnessed an inflationary situation as well as a scarcity of metals that had to be imported. It was in this context of rising prices that minting of the copper pie was discontinued after 1942.

Ten years later, there was a proposal by the Mint Master that the pie be reintroduced as a part of the coinage of Republic India. The proposal, however, was very gently squashed by the then Finance Secretary, Shri K.G. Ambegaonkar on cost-benefit considerations. Ambegaonkar later also served as Governor of the Bank for about a month in 1957. C.D. Deshmukh, the former Governor of the Bank, was then the Finance Minister. He as "Minister" wrote the last word ending the saga of the humble pie.

Ambegaonkar stated:

Much as I admire the valiant efforts made to rescue the 'picayune coin', I must, I am afraid, albeit with a heavy heart, write:

The Epitaph of the Pie
>   Low and high
>   We all will sigh
>   When the poor little pie
>   Bids her last goodbye.
>
>   But her cost's is so high;
>   And what can she buy?
>   What trade can she ply?
>   She needs must eat the humble pie;
>
>   So let us not vie
>   To keep alive the pie
>   And without a plaintive cry
>   Peacefully let her die.
>
>   If you want the reason why
>   There need not be hue and cry
>   Remember she'll in honour lie
>   With the silver rupee high!
>   Will the "Minister" say the last word?

(K.G. Ambegaonkar)
Secretary
12 July 1952

In the note, C.D. Deshmukh concurred stating,

>   Let not the 'press' of men
>   Disturb a museum piece
>   When life's extinct, oh then
>   The pie shall lie in peace.

C.D. Deshmukh
13 July 1952

PART-IV

Book Reviews

List of Book Reviews

1. The Reserve Bank of India-Volume 4—1981-1997—History.

2. Mint Road Milestones by Bazil Sheikh, Ranjeeta Dubey and Surendra Khot.

3. Perspectives on Central Banking: Governors Speak.

4. Regional Economy of India—Growth and Finance, Edited by Deepak Mohanty.

5. Challenges to Central Banking in the Context of Financial Crisis, Edited by Subir Gokarn.

6. Money, Finance, Political Economy: Getting it Right by Deena Khatkhate.

7. Indian Economy—A Retrospective View by Manu Shroff, Edited by Deena Khatkhate.

8. Of Economics, Policy and Development—An Intellectual Journey by I.G. Patel.

9. Emerging India by Bimal Jalan.

10. Economic Policies and India's Reform Agenda: New Thinking by Y.V. Reddy.

11. India and the Global Financial Crisis by Dr. Y.V. Reddy.

12. Global Crisis, Recession and Uneven Recovery by Y.V. Reddy.

13. Windows of Opportunity: Memoirs of an Economic Adviser by K.S. Krishnaswamy.

14. Monetary Policy in a Globalized Economy by Rakesh Mohan.

15. Growth with Financial Stability: Central Banking in an Emerging Market by Rakesh Mohan.

16. Financial Policies and Everyday Life by S.S. Tarapore.

17. Interpreting Financial Policies for the Common Person by S.S. Tarapore.

18. Perspectives on Development: Memories of a Development Economist by V.V. Bhatt.

19. A Better India, A Better World by N.R. Narayana Murthy.

20. Reinventing Development Economics: Explorations from the Indian Experiment by N.A. Mujumdar.

21. Growth and Finance—Essays in Honour of C. Rangarajan Edited by Sameer Kochhar.

22. Monetary Governance in Search of New Space by A. Vasudevan.

23. Managing Risks in Commercial and Retail Banking by Amalendu Ghosh.

24. Microfinance in India: Issues, Problems and Prospects: A Critical Review of Literature by Dr. S.L. Shetty.

25. Microfinance for Macro Change Emerging Challenges by Dr Deepali Pant Joshi.

26. Politics Trumps Economics: The Interface of Economics and Politics in Contemporary India by Bimal Jalan and Pulapre Balakrishnan.

27. Monetary Policy, Sovereign Debt and Financial Stability: The New Trilemma, Edited by Deepak Mohanty.

Book Reviews

The Reserve Bank of India-Volume 4—1981-1997

Published by Academic Foundation and Reserve Bank of India;
Pages 1348; Price ₹ 2195

The Reserve Bank of India (RBI) and Academic Foundation deserve the readers' thanks for bringing out the latest volume of RBI History in two volumes. The earlier histories were fat and unwieldy single tomes.

The RBI is one of the few Central Banks to have documented its institutional history. The book under review is the 4th volume of the history of RBI and relates to the 16-year period (1981-1997). During this period, RBI had six Governors for different terms—Dr I.G. Patel, Dr Manmohan Singh, Shri A. Ghosh, Shri R.N. Malhotra, Shri S. Venkitaramanan and Dr C. Rangarajan.

To recapitulate, there have been three volumes of the History. The 1st volume relates to the period 1935 to 1951 and deals with the steps taken to create a Central Bank for India. It is an account of the birth of RBI which started functioning from 1 April 1935. The hurdles faced by both the Government and the Bank during the Second World War and the initial years of Independence are vividly captured in this volume. The 2nd volume relates to the next 16 years from 1951 to 1967, which was when an era of planned development had been ushered in. It depicts graphically the developments leading to a tough external payments position and the first ever devaluation of the Indian rupee. The period 1967 to 1981—yet another slot of 16 years covered in the 3rd volume deals with a matter of paramount significance in Indian economic history—the nationalisation of 14 banks in 1969. During this period, banking really spread throughout the country. The 1971 withdrawal of the Bretton Woods system put all in a quandary and India was one of those countries considerably affected. Co-ordination between Government and the RBI assumed great importance. All these problems are portrayed clearly in this volume.

The period of the 4th volume under review—1981-1997—is one of the most challenging periods for our economy. The volume takes us through the difficult times when the RBI and Government had to battle with unprecedented strains on the external payments position. The Government embarked on a wide-ranging programme of economic reforms that defined a marked re-orientation of the philosophy of economic management of the country.

This volume was prepared under the guidance of an Advisory Committee headed by Dr Bimal Jalan, former Governor. He was assisted by Dr Subir Gokarn, Dr Rakesh Mohan, Dr A. Vasudevan, Dr Amitava Bose, and Dr Dilip Nachane. Shri Deepak Mohanty, Executive Director, closely monitored preparation of the volume.

The volume under review is in two parts—Part A and Part B—in order to be treated as a continuous narration. Part A tackles the movement from an era of restrictions to one which witnessed progressive liberalisation. What stood out during this period was an expansionary fiscal policy dovetailed by automatic monetisation of budgetary deficits that inevitably imposed a constraint on monetary policy. Efficiency of the banking system was impaired by heavy regulation. A full-fledged balance of payment (BoP) crisis overtook the country in 1991, aided and abetted by domestic macroeconomic imbalances together with deteriorating external conditions. This led to the inauguration of far reaching changes, both in the economy and in central banking.

Part B is a story of reforms. It recounts the initiation of structural and financial sector reforms; fiscal changes of a corrective nature; and phasing out of automatic monetisation. Steps were taken to develop the Government securities market and ensure strong integration of money, securities and foreign exchange markets. Also covered is the change in banking leading to liberalisation and improvement in credit delivery. Like a miasma, the Securities Scam had cast an ugly shadow on the banking system and eventually resulted in better control measures. The payments and settlement systems were also strengthened by innovative measures.

The year 1991 represented a major shift in economic and financial policies, following the balance of payments crisis. Using this as base, the sequence of events covered in this volume is distinguished in two distinct phases. The first phase covering the period 1981-1989 marked as 'Consolidation and Early Liberalisation'. The second, covering 1989-1997 is designated as 'Crisis and Reforms'.

Developments during the 1980s in the areas of monetary management, banking and financial institutions, external sector, rural credit and supervisory practices are succinctly covered. The 1980s was an inward looking, planned and administered era, though several attempts were made at liberalising some segments of the economy. During this decade, India encountered enormous uncertainties. Fiscal dominance acted as a constraint to manoeuvrability of monetary policy implementation. Attempts were made at creating a systematic institutional infrastructure for rural credit with the establishment of National Bank for Agriculture and Rural Development (NABARD) in 1982. Steps were taken to develop financial markets, particularly the money market since the mid-1980s.

The second part of the volume portrays how at the turn of 1990s, the country grappled with several uncertainties such as fragile economic circumstances and political unease that called for firm policy actions. India faced an unprecedented BoP crisis in 1991. On fiscal front, a challenge confronted the economy. The need of the hour was fiscal correction, monetary stability, inflation control and regaining competitiveness.

The economic reforms of 1991 were implemented in a gradual and cautious manner and enabled India to gain credibility internationally. Devaluation of the rupee in 1991 gave a fillip to exports. This combined with wide-ranging liberalisation efforts in various sectors helped to restore macroeconomic balance in the economy. The RBI gained greater space for monetary operations after the agreement with the Government in 1994 so as to phase out the issue of ad hoc Treasury Bills and discontinue automatic monetisation of deficit by March 1997.

Notably there was significant organisational evolution of the RBI. The changes in the composition of the RBI, signifying its structural transformation have been detailed with its functional progression, since the Bank was called upon to play a unique role for addressing the challenges posed by the circumstances.

Four important Committees played a crucial role during this period. The Committee to review the monetary system headed by Prof Sukhamoy Chakravarty transformed the policy paradigm with respect to the objectives of monetary policy, regulation over money and credit, interest rates policy and co-ordination of monetary and fiscal policies. The implementation of the Narasimham Committee report for financial sector reform led to far-reaching changes. Guidelines were issued for income recognition, asset classification, provisioning by RBI and timely adoption of the Basel Accord of capital adequacy standards. The Janakiraman Committee brought into sharp focus deficiencies present in the functioning of the financial system and emphasised the lack of internal control mechanisms following the Securities Scam in 1992. The Vaghul Committee provided a detailed procedural roadmap in the context of strengthening the institutional structure instruments and operating procedures to widen and deepen the money market.

The book is not only a historical account of the Central Bank's past, but throws a flood of light also on the country's economic programmes and policies during the relevant period. The two volumes are extremely well produced with an attractive layout and kudos are due to the co-publishers, Academic Foundation.

•

Mint Road Milestones by Bazil Sheikh, Ranjeeta Dubey and Surendra Khot

Published by Reserve Bank of India;
Pages 476; Price ₹ 1650

The period between April 2009 and March 2010 was the Platinum Jubilee year of the RBI, which commenced operations on 1 April 1935. The RBI has rightly celebrated the entire year with a variety of events such as release of PJ stamps, release of special PJ coins, outreach programmes at schools, colleges and villages, lectures by eminent persons, discussions, etc. One of these worthy of high praise is publishing of the *Mint Road Milestones*, a coffee table book copiously illustrating the history of RBI. The Bank has earlier released three volumes on its history with exhaustive and exhausting reading material aimed at the student and the scholar.

Governor Dr Subbarao in a Foreword to the book under review declares:

> The Bank has been at the forefront of building public policy and economic thought. Its story, in some ways reflects the story of finance and banking in India...This retrospective gives a glimpse into the Bank's eventful past and the road it has traversed. The journey is supported by visuals and vignettes that transcend time to bring alive the spirit of one of the oldest central banks of the developing world.

An introductory chapter furnishes a cogent and abbreviated history of the Bank, beginning with the Hilton Young Commission, the efforts of J.M. Keynes, the Central Banking Enquiry Committee Report, etc. The RBI Act came into force on 1 January 1935. The first Governor was Sir Osborne Smith, an Australian who resigned before his term was over. We have been furnished details of how RBI was transformed from a private shareholders' bank to a fully Government owned institution. The slow, sure and steady enlargement of its functions led to new areas such as agriculture, industry, economic development and financial inclusion. Covered are the devaluation of the Rupee, demonetisation of high-value currency notes, exchange control regulations, establishment of several bodies such as Unit

Trust of India (UTI), Industrial Development Bank of India (IDBI), Agricultural Refinance and Development Corporation (ARDC), etc. All these innovations were in addition to its traditional role of issue of currency, debt management, etc. A primary concern of the Bank was the development of a tremendous database with a variety of publications like the Annual Report, the Currency and Finance Report and the valuable monthly bulletins. The Bank provides a cornucopia of valuable and accurate information on vital aspects of our economy.

The period of 75 years is divided in this volume into six phases. The first period—1935-1949 covers the years up to nationalisation of RBI and the legislation of Banking Companies Act. The first era of planning (1950-1968) forms the essence of the next section and includes establishment of new institutions so as to build a fresh financial architecture for the country. The crucial event of bank nationalisation and its aftermath is the subject matter of the third period (1969-1981) which was plagued by a nightmarish external payments position and witnessed our resort to International Monetary Fund (IMF) loan. The period 1982-1990 was the era of liberalisation, especially after mid-1980s. The year 1991 spelt crisis and became the stage to opt for opening up of the economy toward a market economy. It covered the years 1991-2000.The final phase is dedicated to the new millennium (2001-2009) and shows how reforms were consolidated and the country moved over to achieve strikingly higher growth rates.

A timeline of events very skillfully summarises the major world events throughout the volume. International events of significance are provided in a capsule form. This includes not merely banking developments, but other arenas too. A few examples will illustrate the gamut of this successful attempt. Black Tuesday or when the United States (US) stock exchange collapsed (1929), the Royal Indian Naval Mutiny (1946), Bandung Conference (1955), launching of Sputnik (1957), Martin Luther King's outstanding oration—"I Have A Dream..."(1963), Mother Teresa being awarded the Nobel Prize and the Bharat Ratna (1997; 1980), and Barack Obama becoming America's first-ever Black President (2009). All the Nobel Laureates in Economics are covered with their photographs. This work of highlighting major events is meticulously done and is highly commendable.

The RBI, as stated earlier, has published three volumes of its authorized history covering the period up to 1981. These are serious tomes for the scholars and students. The volume under review will attract not only students, but also the lay public—the vast number of individuals thirsting to improve their knowledge and widen their vision.

There are three chapters worthy of special mention. One is devoted to all the 22 Governors beginning with Sir Osborne Smith to the latest incumbent Dr D. Subbarao. One paragraph is allotted to each Governor, recounting the highlights of his tenure. We have excellent portraits of all the Governors. Another chapter deals with all the buildings owned by the Bank at various centres including the three training colleges in Mumbai, Chennai and Pune. There is a hilarious account of the statues of Yaksha and Yakshini on two sides of the entrance to the RBI New Delhi office building. Questions were raised in the Parliament about the Yaksha and the Yakshini. The Yaksha bore an uncanny resemblance to a Bombay politician Sadobha Patil. In fact, the statue is that of Kuber, the God of wealth. The Yakshini, which was described as the statue of a semi-naked woman, is the representation of agriculture and prosperity.

The chapter "Lives and Times at the Bank" is surely bound to excite nostalgia with rare and unobtainable photos of persons, groups and events during this long period. Special mention must be made of the inclusion of the photo of Subedar Sam Bahadur who worked with several Governors and who came in for special praise by Governor H.V.R. Iengar, who paid tribute to Sam Bahadur's "Dharma".

Admirable is the tremendous effort involved in ferreting out newspapers of these 75 long years and providing photostat copies of the reports on major events. Also one is entertained by the original reaction of two of India's greatest cartoonists Shankar Pillai and R.K. Laxman, who employ their pungent wit to comment on many a development.

A couple of omissions deserve to be highlighted. During the 1993 serial Mumbai blasts, three officers of the Bank, belonging to Department of Banking Operations and Development (DBOD), lost their lives while inspecting a foreign bank in the Air India building. It is a matter for deep regret that there is no mention of this great sacrifice in this volume. In fact the volume should have been dedicated to these three officers as well as those who lost their lives during service in RBI. A matter of minor regret is the failure to mention in the section on Governors of the Bank that seven of them have been conferred by GoI the national awards, Padma Vibhushan/Padmabhushan.

The Governor and his team of editors deserve to be warmly complimented in bringing out this excellent compendium, which is an easy-to-absorb capsule history of our Central Bank and the Indian economy for 75 years with a backdrop of international events. It is a veritable feast to the eyes and rich repast to the brain.

•

Perspectives on Central Banking: Governors Speak
Published by Reserve Bank of India;
Pages 498; Price ₹ 1400

The Platinum Jubilee of an institution is the most appropriate occasion to review its genesis, growth and prospects. This has been eloquently achieved by the book under review which was released by Dr Manmohan Singh, himself a Governor of RBI (1982-1985). Undoubtedly, this book provides an appreciation of the RBI's chequered history and its role in nation building.

The RBI occupies a unique and distinctive place in the Indian banking and financial system. It is the monetary authority and central bank of the country and has been assigned wide powers and responsibilities to overview, develop and regulate the financial system. It was set up in 1935 under the RBI Act, 1934. Initially, its objective was, as the Preamble to the Act states, "to regulate the issue of bank notes with a view to securing monetary stability in India and generally to operate the currency and credit system of the country to its advantage." After Independence, the ownership of the Bank was transferred to the Government and it was assigned a developmental role as well, besides that of regulator of the financial system. It is the banker to banks and also regulator of the activities of banking, non-banking companies and financial institutions in the country.

The main functions of RBI are the issue of bank notes, transaction of government business, managing public debt, undertaking of transactions in foreign exchange as Controller of foreign exchange, keeping of cash reserves of banks, granting loans and advances to scheduled commercial banks and co-operative banks, granting of loans to other financial institutions, granting of advances to Governments, controlling credit and acting as the Regulatory and Supervisory Authority.

This compendium of key speeches of RBI Governors is the RBI's tribute to its past leaders. Seventy-five years is a relatively short span for an institution. Even so, this journey from 1935 has been eventful for the Bank, shaping not only its intellectual evolution but also securing its pre-eminent position in the country's economic policy. This period has witnessed momentous changes—a paradigm shift in economic ideology, ever new perspectives on economic development, growing aspirations of people, path-breaking financial innovations and game-changing technological breakthroughs. All these are changes which considerably influenced the RBI which has responded in its own unique way.

The major events during these 75 years included several important developments, both on the national and the international front. Internationally, the aftermath of the Great Depression of 1930s; the Second World War and the consequent challenges of war financing; the establishment of new International monetary system in 1944; the rule of the gold standard and crude oil price reverberations of 1970s; the Third World debt crisis of 1980s; the Asian crisis of the mid-1990s; and most recently, the global financial turmoil.

Within the country we began with the launching of five-year plans and the stark challenges posed by the most ambitious and gigantic experiments in economic development, the after-effects of the two wars in the 1960s, the devaluation of the rupee in 1966, bank nationalisation in 1969, the BoP crisis of the early 1990s and the follow on path-breaking economic reforms that marked a paradigm shift in our economic policy. The RBI has played its role admirably in addressing these developments, responding to them with sensitivity, professionalism and integrity.

The high esteem in which the RBI is held today owes much to the intellectual leadership and vision of successive Governors. The speeches in this compendium are a testimony to that. They mark a journey through time and provide a glimpse into the ideas, issues and concerns that were inextricably intertwined with the RBI over this period.

The wide-ranging themes covered by the speeches—monetary policy, external sector management, issues in the financial sector and the real economy, economic development and poverty reduction, regulation of banks and financial markets and challenges of managing economic policy in a globalising environment—indicate clearly the role played by the RBI and its continued commitment towards public good.

The basic objectives of economic policy have remained roughly the same: growth with stability and social justice. The RBI has played a very important role in drawing the attention of our country to make our credit system more sensitive to the needs of our farmers and our rural community. It was instrumental in setting up several institutions and diversifying the financial system. The present, more inclusive financial system owes a great deal to the innovative ideas emerging from the RBI.

The RBI had 22 Governors from the first Australian Osborne Smith to the latest Dr Duvvuri Subbarao. The terms of Governors have varied from eight years to just 22 days. Some Governors did not make a speech and the book under review has 32 speeches by 18 Governors.

The speeches and the quotes are embellished with the track history of India's economy. Obviously, in a brief review, one cannot cover all the speeches. We select a few. The first Indian Governor C.D. Deshmukh's speeches are noted for their extraordinary clarity, felicity of expression and grace of style. His lecture on 'Central Banking in India: A Retrospect' is a racy account of the evolution of the Bank, the deliberations at Bretton Woods, the pow-wows between the Finance Member and the RBI authorities on the inflationary situation following depression, the rupee-shilling ratio and his own appointment as Governor. Deshmukh's description of his predecessor James Taylor is worth recalling, "His intelligence was like a lambent flame which illumined everything that it touched and purged it of dross, and he had a catholicity of interest, a breadth of outlook and a warm humanity which I have seldom seen equalled ."

Shri P.C. Bhattacharyya was the Governor when the Indian rupee was devalued. In his B.F. Madon Memorial lecture on 'Monetary Policy and Economic Development', he offers a masterly analysis of the objectives of monetary policy so devised that distribution of credit conforms to the pattern of investment. Monetary policy—the Governor had stressed—must concern itself with the appropriate qualitative influence on productive activity. It is an inalienable aspect of the state's intervention in the economic process and must naturally be attuned to the larger economic objectives of the state.

Perhaps the most visionary Governor was Dr Manmohan Singh. During his tenure, comprehensive legal reforms of the banking sector led to the introduction of a new chapter in the Reserve Bank of India Act. His speech on 'Indian Banking System in the Seventh Five Year Plan' is a thorough analysis of the problems faced by the banking industry, the challenges and the opportunities and the need to change structures, systems, procedures and work practices that will ensure that the banks successfully discharge their expanded responsibilities.

We are led to the groves of academe as we read the two speeches of Dr C. Rangarajan, a distinguished member of IIM. The M.G. Kutty memorial lecture on "Autonomy of Central Banks" is a scintillating analysis of the background to autonomy of the central banks in foreign countries. We are then led on, step by step, typical of an IIM Professor, about the Indian experience from the days of Sir Jeremy Raisman, nationalisation and its aftermath, the Chakravarty Committee report, etc. Autonomy, declared Dr Rangarajan, is not unrestrained. In a democratic set-up, it can and will always be subject to policy directives either from the Government or the legislature.

A heartwarming lecture included in the volume is the one given by Dr Y.V. Reddy to the villagers of Karamchedu, originally delivered in Telugu. He explained in simple terms "What RBI means to the Common Person". Using simple terms the Governor advised the villagers what they can expect from such a powerful institution. This shows the human face of RBI.

This compendium provides an appreciation of the RBI's eventful history and its contribution to nation building. It also highlights the RBI's need to pursue the frontiers of knowledge even as it remains sensitive to the core concerns of the emergent market economy, but one which is still home to crores of poor people.

•

Regional Economy of India: Growth and Finance
Edited by Deepak Mohanty
Published by Academic Foundation and Reserve Bank of India;
Pages 508; Price ₹ 1095

One of the favourable developments in the field of 'economic literature' is the collaboration between Academic Foundation and the RBI, resulting in a series of books that throw a flood of light on banking, economics and our economy. The book under review is the latest and is edited by Shri Deepak Mohanty, an Executive Director of the Bank. He is in charge of monetary policy, economic research and statistics.

Strategies of regional growth and related issues are of paramount importance in overall economic policy both in developing and developed countries. According to Governor Dr Subbarao, analysis of regional economics has assumed importance for three reasons. Disparities across and within regions have noticeably widened. What decides economic growth is higher productivity of firms and workers dependent on a tiny number of regional clusters. While human and geographical distances have been abridged by close regional integration, there has been an undeniable widening of economic distance.

RBI economists have conducted intensive research on regional economy and this book is the culmination of their intellectual exercise aided by rich practical experience. We are offered remarkable insights into regional development experiences.

RBI conducts a number of surveys and gleans data on developments in regional economy. Based on this, the economists prepare analytical studies, which are now made available to the public. The book is divided into five sections. The first section is devoted to growth and inflation and has five chapters. The introductory chapter tackles inclusive growth and its regional dimension. Detailed analysis is made of topics such as male-female literary gap, infant mortality rates, rural and urban population, gender disparity and unemployment. Growth rate in agriculture has been the lowest and most volatile; growth in industry has less variability, while growth in services improved sharply. Distribution of bank credit has been uneven across the sectors and regions. A faster rate of growth must be achieved in agriculture and there ought to be higher absorption of labour in the manufacturing sector. There is a crying need for expansion in social security schemes for the unorganised workers. The study underscores the significance of the role that bank credit plays in financing private investment. There are three papers on 'Impact of Bank Credit on Growth Dynamics of Kerala'; 'Determinants of Inflation in Tamil Nadu' and 'Inter-District Growth Performance in Madhya Pradesh.' The Editor's lecture in Gauhati University on economic developments in Northeastern states finds a place in this section.

The second section is dedicated to Banks and Finance. The first paper on micro-finance declares that the pattern of development of this sector has been highly skewed as poorer regions remain under-served. It has a long way to go to attain further social objectives of fostering financial inclusion. There is an urgent need to provide both demand and supply impetus to the micro-finance sector. According to four economists who discuss the regional dimensions of banking services— on the sole basis of savings bank accounts—the Southern region has the most banking facilities; this is grossly inadequate in Northeastern, Central and Eastern regions. Both RBI and the Government have taken measures to enlarge financial inclusion. One paper studies 'Bank finance in Development of Real Estate sector in Bihar' and records certain improvements. The impact of monetary policy on dispersion of credit is the subject of a third paper. This parameter varies from state to state. Only infra-structural development will influence credit dispersion in a desirable way.

The third section comprises three contributions on financial inclusion. Progress in Jammu and Kashmir is studied with comparisons through a 'Financial Inclusion Index.' Chandigarh, Delhi and Goa rank high, while Jammu and Kashmir scores very low. Kerala leads with the highest level followed by Maharashtra and Karnataka. The success in Kerala is attributed to the high level of awareness among people about the benefits of financial inclusion.

The last section is concerned with structural issues. The study on Punjab highlights the need for the state to re-position itself so as to strengthen the economic structure. Budgetary operations of the state governments are analysed thoroughly and social expenditure of 16 major states are studied. The need to re-prioritise expenditure by the states by giving preference to public and merit goods is emphasised. The case study on Delhi reveals that the share of services in employment is close to its share in output, unlike the all-India position. A study of the realty sector during 1999 to 2009 revealed a decline in the primary sector and betterment in the service sector. Credit played a greater role in deciding the demand for housing credit across the states. Debt management strategies in Uttar Pradesh (UP) and Uttarakhand have led to distinct achievements and their reform process, and debt management strategies have enhanced their fiscal sustainability.

The lessons from these valuable studies is that while the share of agriculture sector has shrunk, that of the services sector has expanded. Serious attention needs to be paid to the former. There is a distinct need to improve industrial climate and infrastructure. Sustained efforts are called for reducing disparities between the developed and undeveloped districts. Social sector has a greater role to play. Outreach of banking services has to expand faster.

Without doubt, tremendous hard work and extensive thinking has gone into this seminal volume. Only if regional development is satisfactory, the entire nation can advance. All articles are ably supported by statistical tables, figures and charts as also rich references. The book cries out for an index. Academic Foundation and the RBI deserve our gratitude for bringing out such a valuable volume.

•

Challenges to Central Banking in the context of Financial Crisis
Edited by Subir Gokarn
Published by Reserve Bank of India and Academic Foundation;
Pages 492; Price ₹ 1295

The RBI celebrated its Platinum Jubilee during 2009-2010 and as a part of its celebration organised an International Research Conference in Mumbai. The papers and proceedings of the Conference have been brought out in this new book edited by Deputy Governor Subir Gokarn. The theme of the Conference was 'Challenges to Central Banking in the context of the Financial Crisis'. The inaugural address was made by Governor Subbarao followed by a keynote speech by the Nobel Laureate Andrew Michael Spence of Stanford University; four technical sessions were held and papers were presented and discussed.

There are in all 36 contributors, including seven Central Bank Governors and six Deputy Governors and a galaxy of bankers, economists and professors. The volume offers the distilled wisdom of recognised academicians, policymakers and central bankers. It analyses thoroughly, *inter alia*, problems like monetary policy, debt crisis, exchange rate policies, financial stability imperatives, etc.

According to Governor Subbarao, who effectively poses the problems, there are five key challenges to all central banks. The first one is managing national monetary policy decisions in a globalised environment. The second is redefining the mandate of the central bank in the context of inflation targeting and asset prices. The third challenge is central bank responsibility to maintain financial stability. The fourth is the ability to manage costs and benefits of regulation. The final challenge is the need for autonomy and accountability of central banks.

The Nobel Laureate economist, Prof Spence was the Chairman of the Commission of Growth and Development. The Commission was formed chiefly by political and public policy leaders from the developing world. According to him, 13 countries grew at the rate of 7 per cent or more over 25 years. India and Vietnam are likely to join this group in the near future. Two factors responsible for this was maintenance of a stable macroeconomic environment conducive to investment, and a high level of investment made including public sector investment. A key component of high growth was the very heavy investment in human capital. Prof Spence averred that central banks have an informative advantage because of the work they do. They have, in addition, a capital advantage—much as an entity like the IMF has—and that is superb analytical talent. He laid emphasis on four factors—managing inflation, internal and external crises, volatility and achieving autonomy without losing credibility.

The technical sessions discussed threadbare issues like policy discretion, regulatory systems flexible inflation targeting and asset prices'. Another subject was the challenges posed by globalisation to central banks and fiscal problems of industrial countries. The third session concentrated on disruptions in financial systems and the imperative need for financial stability mandate. Regulatory responses should not be allowed to stifle financial innovations. The fourth session examined whether financial stability should be an explicit objective of monetary policy and whether its absence contributed to the financial crisis.

In the two panel discussions, Governors of the central banks offered their candid views on important issues with both country and global perspective. Five critical issues related to the international monetary system were the subject of discussion in a panel. The discussions were given direction by the Deputy Governors of RBI, who also offered a summing-up.

Quoting from the latest book of Niall Ferguson, The Ascent of Money, Governor Subbarao stated: "Sometimes the most important historical events are the non-events: the thing that did not occur." The spectacular non-event of the crisis is that the Great Recession did not turn into the Great Depression. For this, central bankers should get a part of the credit.

This is a volume to be read with great care and diligence. It contains the essence of wisdom of some of the wisest heads of our generation. Among the distinguished participants were Martin Wolf, Chief commentator of Financial Times, William Pole, Federal Reserve Bank of St.Louis, John Lipsky, Deputy Managing Director of the IMF and B. Friedman, Professor, Harvard University. The RBI and the Academic Foundation deserve praise for making the valuable proceedings of the conference available to students, scholars, bankers, economists, planners and the public.

•

Money, Finance, Political Economy: Getting It Right
by Deena Khatkhate
Published by Academic Foundation (2009);
Pages 386; Price ₹ 995

Deena Khatkhate is a world-renowned economist who was an invaluable part of several prestigious institutions—RBI, IMF, World Bank, the United Nations (UN) and the Asian and African development banks. His articles appeared in journals like *The Quarterly Journal of Economics*, *The Review of Economics and Statistics*, *The Oxford Economic Papers*, *The Oxford Bulletin of Economics and Statistics*, *The Journal of Post Keynesian Economics*, *Economic Development and Cultural Change*, *The Journal of Development Studies*, *The Economic and Political Weekly*, *Social Research*, *World Development*, *Economia Internazionale*, *IMF Staff Papers* etc. He was associate editor of the *Encyclopedia of India* with Stanley Wolpert as the Chief. He was Managing Editor of *World Development*. He has several books to his credit—the latest was *Ruminations of a Gadfly*, one about which Ramachandra Guha proclaimed, "Deena Khatkhate is that rare Indian intellectual who is not captive of an ideology.. his wonderfully wide-ranging collection of essays.. are consistently readable and often provocative—one is always stimulated by the originality of his arguments."

"The Gang of Four" was how Shri M. Narasimham, ex-Governor of the RBI, described in his *From Reserve Bank to Finance Ministry and Beyond: Some Reminiscences*, the 'Brains Trust' of the Research Department of the RBI. The Gang comprised himself, V.V. Bhatt, A.G. Chandavarkar and Deena Khatkhate. Deena was the youngest of the Four Musketeers—an intellectual D'Artagnan! The last three economists went to the IMF and World Bank where they rendered distinguished service and brought out books and reports acclaimed worldwide. All were noted for their brilliant contributions to academic journals. They are the true intellectuals.

The book under review offers further proof to buttress Ramachandra Guha's accolade quoted earlier. It consists of 27 assorted articles published in reputed journals—a few are unpublished—covering national and international aspects of money, finance, and exchange rates and the political economy of development. These pieces written decades ago have proved the author's prognostications, confirmed his fears. He is magnanimous to admit that he was wrong in regard to the impact of fiscal deficit on real interest rates—a quality rarely noted in economists! Lay readers are introduced to the dynamics of monetary theory and finance from the perspective of developing countries and the restraints imposed by political economy on the issues of economic development.

Analysing the Indian political system, the author argues that it operates in such a way that economic policy has punishment as its basis lacking in any sanction for its enforcement, while at the same time providing incentive as its basis without any built-in-mechanism for rewarding success. Such a situation leads unerringly to political opportunism and concentration of power at the centre in a federal polity. The only solution lies in radical transformation diffusing political power to state units—even lower down the line to districts.

Tackling the sensitive problem of 'economic growth *versus* income distribution', Khatkhate reviews ways in which presently the poverty level has sharply declined, though income distribution has not improved as much as desired. This is chiefly due to Governmental failure to translate growth into more equal income distribution. The economist further warns, "Until the transforming leadership evolves with its benign impact on the political process, Indian politicians and bureaucrats will continue to indulge in hoary, futile and wordy debate on equality and growth."

Paul Baran mourned the absence of an "intellectual class" in India and opined that we have only intellectual workers—who despite making significant contribution in social and natural sciences, failed to influence the extent and nature of social and political change in India. The role of intellectuals was pre-empted by leftist ideologues who obfuscated informed debate and attempted to revive discredited policies.

In a stimulating essay on brain drain, Khatkhate argued that "... brain drain provides a safety valve for the less well developed countries which possess surplus university graduates. So long as the tendency to produce these persists, the brain drain is inevitable." He quotes Prof P.C. Mahalanobis, who said that the productivity of statisticians in Indian conditions is low because they operate in a social and institutional environment which stultified their initiative and creativity. Emigration, affirms the author, leads to more invisible earnings, and spread of technology and new ideas to the developing countries. Brain drain has increased trade between emigrating and host countries, foreign direct investment (FDI) and spread of technology.

On the subject of international monetary systems, the author had shown prescience in his articles written in 1987. The ideas he put forth are now being seriously debated in international fora. International institutions like the IMF and World Bank are at the crossroads, in search of a new mission and of a *raison d'etre* for their very existence. The idea—espoused by him—has taken hold that there is a need to decentralise operations of IMF in the context of emerging monetary unions. Some economists have argued for the Federal Reserve System type of organisational structure for IMF. Deena Khatkhate expounds the advantages of having regional monetary arrangements such as the Chiang Mai initiative.

The learned author modestly confesses that he had to recant his views regarding his justification of fiscal deficit for financing economic development. He had believed that fiscal deficit in the presence of large unemployment and excess capacity in the producing sectors would result in new investment without inflationary pressures. Experience of the emerging countries, including India, has demonstrated that the basic assumption that interventionist policies of the state would be effective was unfounded.

The economist concludes that the central theme in money and finance is that a country's monetary policy and system are critical to the pace and nature of the development process. One of India's successful practitioners of planning, Dr Montek Singh Alhuwalia has commented: "This delightful collection of essays spans some of the key issues in monetary and financial policy which have been at the heart of the development policy debate for the past three decades. His analysis reflects extensive insider knowledge and displays continuing relevance." High praise indeed but absolutely well-deserved. The articles of Deena Khatkhate have stood the test of time and are as relevant today as when it was written decades ago.

•

Indian Economy: A Retrospective View by Manu Shroff
Edited by Deena Khatkhate

Published by Academic Foundation;

Pages 286; Price ₹ 795

Manu Shroff was a genuine champion of economic liberalism, who was also an inalienable part of the Indian economic bureaucracy. He asserted his views without fear or favour, as adviser to the Planning Commission, Banking Secretary, member of the Finance Commission, and as Editor of *The Economic Times* (1984-1989). He was an intimate associate of the Gujarat School of Economics, along with distinguished members such as Dr Jagdish Bhagwati, Dr I.G. Patel and Dr Lakdawala. He became the President of Gujarat Economic Association. He was a voracious reader who read *The Economist* and the *Economic and Political Weekly* (EPW) from cover to cover. He was a trusted adviser to Alaknanda, the wife of Dr I.G. Patel in her monumental effort of bringing out the collected works of her father, Professor A.K. Dasgupta.

The book under review is edited by Deena Khatkhate, an eminent economist, who held high positions in RBI, World Bank, IMF and the UN. He is the author of several books. His recent book, *Ruminations of a Gadfly* was highly acclaimed by Ramachandra Guha for "the originality of his arguments and transparent sincerity." That volume included an essay entitled "Manu Shroff: Economist with pride as his carapace", which had originally appeared in EPW and is a fitting tribute to a great but modest economist. When a friend asked Manu Shroff why he had not published his papers in any academic journal of repute, his insouciant reply was: "It does not matter so long as it is there in the literature." Shroff had an original bent of mind without a desire for self-promotion and public adulation. He took his triumphs and travails in stride without rejoicing or remorse, a hallmark of equanimity.

This volume contains Shroff's articles and lectures on several aspects of Indian economy from its highly interventionist regime to a liberalised open economic system, as also a few international issues which affected our economy. The Editor quotes appropriately with approval, Paul Baran who characterised the hallmarks of an intellectual as one who "perceives prevailing social and political reality in its inter-connectedness or as a part of historical progress." Shroff was one true intellectual. He was bright as an economic adviser, which entailed quickness of mind in order to adapt abstract economic ideas to the real world, where considerations of political economy override logical discourse. Shroff was an economic thinker too.

The first part of this book is titled "National Issues" and is focused on the Indian economy with its different dimensions in retrospect, in its current phase, when the pieces were published and in prospect. The second part is on "International Issues" and tackles international monetary matters and globalisation which radicalised the approach towards economic development as distinguished from the unregulated growth that characterised the period up to the 1980s. The Editor discerns a methodological consistency in Shroff's thought process and his basic beliefs.

Shroff argues that owing to the nature of India's polity, a purely market-oriented approach would not work, if not for no other reason than that it would not be acceptable to people. What we have learnt in India is that state intervention can be made more efficient than in the past. An inordinately large amount of time and energy of bureaucrats seems to be devoted to industry and not enough to the more difficult task of blowing the winds of change to the countryside. According to him, India is beginning to learn from its past mistakes and shed time-worn prejudices. Pragmatism has become order of the day.

The author has been prophetic about the Indian economy during the Rajiv Gandhi era. Though he concedes that there was upward growth in the economy, the policy framework built during the initial years of the that era lies tattered and ad-hoc-ism was the order of the day. Short-term political gains took priority over desirable economic changes. It was the prelude to the economic crisis of 1991. In a critical analysis of 'The Economic Crisis of 1991', Shroff lamented that the political situation was fraught with the grim possibility of continued instability, caused not by differences over issues but unconcealed greed for power and patronage. He predicted with uncanny accuracy that the looming crisis would be triggered by the catastrophic developments in India's balance of payments (BoP), derived from reckless foreign borrowing and neglect of industrial efficiency. Truly, 'A Daniel Come To Judgment.'

He welcomed the reforms initiated by Narasimha Rao and Manmohan Singh but entered a caveat—that the agenda was far from complete. To maintain foreign confidence, Shroff advocated a vigorous avoidance of BoP crisis. He had a vision of India 2010, when he gave a lecture on "Crystal-gazing about the Indian Economy".

He believed that our strong industrial base should encourage forays into newer activities such as communications and information technology. In the financial services sector, the potential will improve as the sector reforms progress further. Financial reforms, he argued, cannot be delayed if the dream of rupee convertibility had to be realised. He has been proved right on the dot.

Manu Shroff strongly believed that market forces and technological changes have been far more important in the process of globalisation than conscious decisions of the government. Globalisation has been growth-oriented and inspired technocrats to spawn vigorous new enterprises in fields such as software and consumer goods, which are employment-intensive.

There are three brilliant reviews by Shroff of the books printed by Jagdish Bhagwati, *Essays in Development Economics*; Pranab Bardhan's *The Political Development in India*; and S.S. Tarapore's *India's Financial Policy*. These give us a glimpse of Shroff's versatility, erudition and remarkable facility to communicate. Perhaps the best essay in the book is "A Perspective on International Monetary Issues", which is a classic analysis from the Bretton Woods conference to the Gold Standard and the latest Basle norms.

Shroff impressed everyone by his robust common sense and sound judgment. Manu Shroff had a great sense of humour. In his review of the Tarapore book, he stated: "Readers are told that during the days of the Raj, the Executive lounge of RBI had a regular live band during the lunch hour. Tarapore would have liked the band, if it were still there, to play "Hail to the Chief" on 15 April 1997, so deeply appreciative is he of the last but one pronouncement of Rangarajan on that day." Manu Shroff loved Bach and was very proud of his collection of music, which he had acquired during his years of stay abroad.

We owe a deep debt to the Editor Deena Khatkhate for allowing us a glimpse into the creative writings of a great economist and erudite thinker. This book is a compulsory read for all who want to understand the economic history of our times and those who feel that India ought to be accepted as a global power of the present century. It is warmly commended to all students of economics, politics and Indian economic development.

•

Of Economics, Policy and Development: An Intellectual Journey by I.G. Patel
Published by Oxford University Press;
Pages 456; Price ₹ 1295

"There is a vacant chair at every cabinet meeting of Jawaharlal Nehru. It is reserved for the ghost of Prof. Harold Laski." This famous statement brings out clearly the paramount influence on Indian administration of the London School of Economics (LSE). Dr I.G. Patel was the first professional economist at the helm of the LSE. Patel's brilliant captaincy of LSE led to a coveted KBE—knighthood from the British Queen. He had a wide, all-enveloping grasp, sharpness of intellect, breadth and sweep of understanding, freshness and clarity of views—all these left his audiences spellbound. Patel was recipient of the Padma Vibhushan in 1991. He was an economist of international repute, a brilliant scholar who brought excellence to whatever he touched, a distinguished teacher, and a sensitive administrator.

The book under review is Patel's intellectual journey and is edited by Dr Y.V. Reddy and Dr D.R. Khatkhate—the former was RBI Governor and the latter was closely associated with the IMF and was Editor of *World Development*.

In a brilliant introduction, Khatkhate writes of Patel's versatile intellectual personality roaming with equal ease in his writings and economic adviser's role on the national scene, as well as international which were all inextricably linked with the personal life of this prodigy. Patel made a successful transition from an academic economist to an economic administrator. He was that rare kind of economist who can simultaneously think and act. His grip over economic theory and over the complex facts of economic life was fantastic.

The criterion adopted by the Editors in their selection of the papers, published and unpublished are explained in detail. Patel's articles reveal a tapestry of ideas in the economics of money, trade, balance of payments, economic development and monetary policy. Some of his ideas are relevant even today and apply in full measure to the Indian and the global stage.

The book has 34 chapters and in a brief review we cannot cover all chapters. The chapter on "Demand for money during periods of inflation and stabilization"—written in 1950 was prepared for the IMF and is published for the first time. It investigates the circumstances under which an expansionist monetary policy is appropriate to the stabilisation of the price level in an inflation-ridden economy. Patel presents a succinct historical survey of the monetary policy during stabilisation taking the actual experience of Germany, Austria and Belgium. He argues that it is desirable to expand the money supply, even while attempting to halt an inflation, if we are not to fall into a 'stabilisation crisis'. India followed some of these ideas when it adopted a policy of non-inflationary financing since the Second Five Year Plan.

Two chapters on Gold analyse the elasticity of demand for gold in India, and the core issue of mobilisation of the stock of hoarded gold and flow of gold into the sinews of economic growth. Patel believed that introduction of gold bonds would prove a flop or would make for strong entrenchment in the country of anti-social activities such as tax evasion and smuggling of gold.

Patel's views on Nehruvian socialism are highly original.

> In its concrete achievements, the socialism of the Nehru era can lay claim to a respectable degree of public ownership of the means of production. But the prevailing tone of social behaviour is unmistakably that of acquisitiveness and private profit.

There is a highly impressive framework of the Second Five Year Plan prepared by Patel, which set a direction for the final version.

A chapter entitled "Miscellany" has affectionate memoirs of two British economists—A.C. Pigou and Adam Smith.

The Epilogue by Dr Reddy affirms that the value of this collection lies not only in providing a background of Patel's thinking on various economic issues that confronted India during half a century of freedom, but also evokes reflections on the global economic contemporary theory and current challenges for policymakers. The book is compulsory reading for bankers, students of monetary policy, finance, trade and policies. It is a veritable economic history of India during the first 50 years after Independence.

•

Emerging India by Bimal Jalan
Published by Penguin/Viking;
Pages 307; Price ₹ 599

India is ruled by an ex-RBI Governor and ex-Finance Minister. The Prime Minister's (PM) Economic Advisory Board is headed by another ex-RBI Governor. Yet the nation is teetering on the precipice of economic decline with a reduction in annual growth and burgeoning inflation. Why is the situation so with such a fund of expertise? The book under review is an attempt to solve this riddle.

Dr Bimal Jalan was a distinguished Governor of the RBI from 1997 to 2003. He became a nominated member of the Rajya Sabha. Apart from serving as Chairman of the Economic Advisory Council to the PM, he has held high positions in the Planning Commission, in several ministries and represented our country in the Boards of the IMF and International Board of Reconstruction and Development (IBRD). He has written a number of books, noted for their clarity, conciseness and clear grasp of the problems that plague the nation. His is a voice to be heard with respect.

The book under review is a collection of his selected papers, lectures and a few unpublished notes— relating to the period 1990 to 2010. They provide a bird's eye view of the evolution of India's politics, economics, governance and economic reforms and the lessons for tomorrow. India could boast a couple of years ago of a high reputation as a democracy and a growing global power. But presently, it is riddled with reports of ever-widening corruption, misgovernment and utter despair about the working of its political system. Our future is a big question mark!

In the last two decades, India displayed a capacity to grow faster than ever before, eliminating poverty to a considerable extent. Certain reforms seem imperative now to ensure future success. According to Jalan, the main areas of concern are the growing disjuncture between economics and politics and the emergence of a public-private dichotomy in the growth trajectory, diminishing accountability of the

Executive to the Parliament, rising corruption, the preponderance of criminal elements in politics and the emergence of small regional parties in multi-party coalitions. There is a definite decline in the quality of public administration at all levels. Economic disparities have enlarged and pose a serious threat to unity.

The book is divided into four sections. The first section, with five articles, concentrates on political issues that cry for a solution to ensure that India retains its position as a global power. In view of the so-called "Compulsion of Coalition", our political system is characterised by features not thought of by our Constitution makers. Governments have become non-accountable. Inner party democracy is non-existent. Political corruption has become rampant. An independent judiciary is unable to deliver justice swiftly due to heavy backlog of work. There is a compulsion to create an efficient and transparent administrative mechanism at an arm's length from—Government, besides the need to simplify procedures. Ministries ought to be made more accountable.

The next section is on India's economy, policy and prospects and consists of six essays. India's emergence as a global power is due to our competitive advantage in providing skill-based services to the rest of the world—owing to the infrastructure of technological institutions, skilled workers and low labour costs. One paper analyses the impact of globalisation on India.

The third section on money, finance and banking is the meatiest part of the volume and has seven articles discussing in depth our management of the financial sector during the Asian Crisis and later. Banking ethics are also scrutinised. Jalan suggests that India must remain in the forefront of global regulatory norms in order to ensure soundness of international banking system. Revolutionary changes in banking and consequential impact are analysed succinctly. The economist strongly supports sustained growth with financial stability. Exchange rate management ought to be in the form of a flexible but managed one. The IMF has declared our policy as realistic and competitive.

The concluding section has seven pieces on India's economic reforms. Three of these articles relate to 1974 and 1975 and have a historical value. We must accelerate the pace of banking reforms leading to efficiency of operations and reduction of costs. India must adopt global best practices in the financial sector regulations and adapt these to domestic environment.

Why was India's reform process during the last 40 years limited in scope? These are answered in the article, "The Politics of India's Reforms". What can be reformed and what cannot be gets determined politically. "Compulsion of Coalitions" affects economic reforms. Corruption has enveloped every sector and is a serious threat to the security and well-being of the citizens and is an affront to democratic values. The Lok Sabha has 100 members with proven criminal records.

Jalan concludes on an optimistic note. India has the capacity to realise its full economic potential and become one of the fastest growing countries. This book is a sterling contribution to making this possible.

•

Economic Policies and India's Reform Agenda: New Thinking by Y.V. Reddy
Published by Orient Blackswan;
Pages 275; Price ₹ 550

It is well known that the Indian economy has registered lower growth rates in the last decade. What are the steps to be taken in order to lift the economy from the morass into which it is sinking?

Some of the best and the brightest individuals have thought over this and offered solutions to overcome this impasse. Dr Y.V. Reddy belongs to this elite group. He is the Chairman of the Fourteenth Finance Commission and was the distinguished Governor of the RBI from 2003 to 2008 and virtually buffeted the country from depredations of the global financial crisis. In fact Joseph Stiglitz, the Nobel Laureate in Economics, declared, "If only we had a Y.V. Reddy at the helm, America would not have faced a financial crisis." It is essential to heed the voice of a pundit like Reddy.

This is Dr Reddy's latest book and comprises lectures he delivered at different fora. It tackles the Reforms agenda India has adopted which could possibly ignore the current debates on the latest crisis, the broader policy lessons and the burgeoning uncertainties that envelop the world economy. Reddy's lectures herald new thoughts on economic policies with particular reference to the management of money, finance and external sector. The volume attempts to generate a discussion on the strategies that deserve to be adopted for facilitating development and the revised programme for reforming the economy.

Reddy formulates clearly what ought to be done for achieving a 9-10 per cent annual growth. Firstly, the level of domestic saving should be restored to pre-crisis levels and also it has to be enhanced significantly. Secondly, the climate for investment should be conducive to a domestic investor. Small and medium business should be recognised and their scope for enlarging employment utilised. Vertical economic and social mobility has to be guaranteed. Thirdly, productivity has to be improved and the country should have the capacity to pay for all imports through exports. Fourthly, public sector capacity should be improved to overcome bottlenecks in our social infrastructure. Indian society demands a sense of fairness in public systems. Finally, a stirring call is made to the private sector to ensure healthy standards of governance and ethical conduct. The task of attaining 9-10 per cent growth has to be attended to by both public and private sector.

The book is divided into three parts. Part one on "economic policy" contains seven lectures focused on the macroeconomic policies, starting with governance in central banks and concluding with an essay on new strategies for development. According to the author, RBI has to become "more central than they were before and with an enlarged mandate." Dr Reddy calls upon the international financial institutions to review their approaches regarding public debt management in the light of experience gained from the crisis. Reforms in the financial sector will have to take place with reference to global thinking and development.

The second part of the book—with six essays—is devoted to the financial sector and asserts that it is an integral part of broader economic policies serving the society at large. Dr Reddy has presented a new approach to public sector banking. The current debate on strengthening of regulation of the financial sector should be expanded to cover ownership, governance, competition and regulation. Good and appropriate governance is the key to desirable performance of both the public and private sectors.

The third part on global economy—comprising five essays—is an exposition of new realities confronting developing economies and implications of the global economic developments for India. We have a succinct analysis of the recent global financial crisis, its implications and how it was tackled. Global crisis had unimagined consequences for developing countries. India has emerged as an influential nation in the global community of nations. Two essays deal with the management of capital account which has direct impact on stability of financial institutions and the exchange rate. One essay is devoted to India, European Union (EU) and the world economy. The final essay is on the impact of global economic development and India. Dr Reddy is of the firm view that India has the potential to play an influential role in the global economy because of its diversity in social, economic and political attainments.

The book is an outstanding contribution to the world of development and will be of immense use to planners, bankers, economists and students of economics.

•

India and the Global Financial Crisis by Y.V. Reddy
Published by Orient Blackswan;
Pages 398; Price ₹595

Dr Y.V. Reddy was the 21st Governor of the RBI and served from September 2003 to September 2008. He is presently Emeritus Professor, University of Hyderabad. He was elected as Honorary

Fellow of the LSE. He was a member of the Indian Administrative Service (IAS). He had spent most of his career in the fields of finance and planning. He had served as Secretary, Ministry of Finance, and in other ministries too. He had a six-year term as Deputy Governor and had assumed the office of Governor thereafter. Before joining RBI, he was India's Executive Director on the Board of the IMF. He made significant contributions in the areas of financial sector reforms, trade finance, monitoring of BoP and exchange rate. He has been closely associated with institution building.

His tenure as Governor for five years was marked by rapid growth of the Indian economy as also extraordinary challenges for the conduct of monetary policy. His role as Governor won international acclaim for managing India's calibrated financial integration with the global economy. His term was characterised by the highest average growth rate achieved by the Indian economy and the lowest average inflation since Independence. Reddy's book is a compilation of 23 speeches that he delivered at various fora in India and abroad in past years. What makes this book interesting is its introduction and epilogue. While the 30-page epilogue talks about the global financial crisis and India, the 34-page introduction explains in the contexts in which these speeches were delivered and Reddy's compulsions. The context for most of the speeches was provided by the serious differences between the finance ministry and the central bank on many critical issues, but Reddy is cautious in his revelations. He has described his differences with the powers-that-be as 'creative tension'.

One of the instances that Reddy cites in his book, lauding the government for the "unstinted support" that was "critical" in strengthening the banking sector, refers to the finance ministry's acceptance of the fact that RBI should have the last word on an issue such as foreign investment in a holding company of a large private sector bank. His introduction says: "The government approved select foreign investments in a holding company structure with respect to a large private sector bank, which was itself a conglomerate with commanding foreign ownership; however this was subject to the approval of the RBI."

The large private bank which is India's largest private sector lender planned to float an intermediate holding company for its insurance and mutual fund businesses and even sold a substantial stake in the proposed holding company to a few foreign investors. The government approved the plan and even the Foreign Investment Promotion Board (FIPB) that deals with overseas investments in local firms cleared the proposed investment by foreign funds in this venture. This was done despite RBI's strong reservations; the central bank felt that such an innovative structure could not be supervised adequately. With extreme reluctance, the finance ministry had to accept RBI's wish to form a working group to look into the proposal. However, the working group frustrated the bank and prospective foreign investors in the venture before declaring it as not 'desirable'. Reddy's version does not convey the friction between the ministry and the central bank, with RBI sticking to its stand.

Y.V. Reddy's book is set against the backdrop of the global economic and financial crisis. After completing his term as Governor of the RBI, in September 2008, he had no specific intention of writing a book and planned to join academia. However, as the crisis intensified, the resilience of the Indian economy and its banks came to be noticed across the world. As the central bank Governor, Dr Reddy had commented on some key features of the global economy that were causing concern in many countries. Sound financial sector regulation had helped the Indian economy to weather the storm. There has been a keen interest across the globe in knowing more about India.

According to Reddy, the unfolding global financial crisis evoked interest among intellectuals not only in the countries affected the most, but also in those, such as India and Canada, which have coped better. India's financial sector regulation was praised. After that, he started receiving a large number of enquiries from various parts of the world. That was when he chose to explain the thought process that went into the policies at that time relating to the external sector and finance. The idea behind the book was to explain the context in which a particular speech was made. Reddy explains the context of the speeches in greater detail now than was possible earlier because of the market's sensitivity to policy announcement and changes. The global imbalances were quite obvious. The asset bubble was also in evidence—prices of shares and real estate were soaring everywhere. The question was how would these imbalances impact. According to one of the views, the market will correct itself. Regulating the markets means that policymakers are assuming a superior wisdom. Policymakers had come under fire. According to that view, markets set the price. It is not for regulators to say that the risks are under priced. When the RBI raised risk weights and provisioning requirements for real estate loans by banks, there was a hue and cry. In international forums, where there have been similar points of criticism, Reddy had pointed out the following: India is a poor, developing country without any social safety network, therefore, a lot of importance is attached to stability and it could not allow the financial system to take too many risks. Banks are special because they are the only place where individuals can safely park their savings. They are built on trust. It is necessary to convince the people as well that banks are safe. It is too high a risk to the entire financial system that a bank should be allowed to fail. The third principle on which regulation is based is that financial markets are not an end by themselves, especially in the case of asset financing; their externalities are huge. The other set of reforms is in the context of global imbalance. A number of people wanted larger foreign investment in India which means a higher current account deficit leading to greater dependence on sources from abroad. This makes us more vulnerable to uncertainties. Our current account deficit should be moderate. In the context of the ongoing global debate on imbalance, our position has been vindicated. Unlike the United States (US) or China, India has only a moderate current account imbalance. The purpose of the financial sector is to help the real sector and it is certainly not an end in itself. Globalisation insofar, as it is related to trade in goods and services, has had beneficial effects. But the distinction between globalisation in general and particularly of the financial sector has presently come to the fore. The key question now is how to manage the globalisation of finance so as to enhance the benefits while minimising its risks. Here we have a basic conflict between national regulation and global regulation. The problem with finance is it is footloose. There cannot be any rules of origin and it becomes very difficult to have "circuit breakers".

Market orientation has helped significantly, but two types of doubts have emerged. First, it has increased inequalities. Secondly, financialisation of markets—when markets became an end in themselves. According to the Governor, there is no incentive for good performance in the public sector banks (PSBs). The government banks have attracted top talent. It is only recently that the new private banks have come up. While handling some new financial products and services, PSBs may be found to not have the skills and the culture. In the ongoing crisis, the best private sector banks have been affected, but the public sector banks have come out unscathed. Regulation in India has to be on the basis of an assessment of the market participants themselves. Over the last 4-5 years, capabilities of the PSBs have strengthened. Most of the innovation has been made towards avoiding the regulatory capital; ways to save on capital; and ways to adopt for maximising profits with the given capital. One has to draw a distinction between good financial innovation and bad financial innovation. The former category benefits society. The latter is merely meant for circumventing financial regulation.

The book is divided into seven sections dealing with indian economy, financial sector reforms, banking sector reforms, monetary policy in a globalising world, organisation and communication policies of the RBI, capital account liberalisation, and global financial imbalances and crisis. Dr Reddy has provided a valuable 10-page bibliography. The book is of tremendous topical value and as Narayana Murthy has aptly summed up, Dr Reddy has an extraordinary ability to explain complex macroeconomic concepts in simple language.

•

Global Crisis, Recession and Uneven Recovery by Y.V. Reddy
Published by Orient Blackswans;
Pages 421; Price ₹ 595

Dr Y.V. Reddy was the 21ˢᵗ Governor of the RBI. He has several publications to his credit relating to finance, planning and public enterprises. We had earlier reviewed his book *India and the Global Financial Crisis*. The book under review is a sequel.

During his five years as Governor, Dr Reddy introduced a number of measures which ensured that India could escape the heat of the meltdown. He had as early as 2006 issued a note of warning of the global crisis and believed that India ought to focus on infrastructure, strengthen its social sector and concentrate on weaknesses in the financial sector. In India, excessive capital inflows may come into the equity and commodity markets, leading to prices shooting up and inflationary pressures.

The book under review contains 27 speeches marked by admirable lucidity and utter clarity. There is a critical analysis of the role of central banks in the evolution of the global financial crisis, with special attention to developing countries. There is potential for a fundamental rebalancing in economic and financial management in the future in the backdrop of the crisis. Dr Reddy points out the serious erosion of public trust in the financial sectors. The financial crisis has spilled over into the economic, social and political arena. Failure of capitalism and reduced bargaining power of labour aggravated inequalities. Constant re-balancing of several forces has led to acute distress. The global crisis represents a failure of that specific model of capitalism marked by exclusive faith in the markets. The most important cause of the global financial crisis was the world of globalised finance with its unclear ethical foundations, domination by global financial conglomerates and considerations of political economy in the international financial centres. The author envisages a shift in the balance in Asia. But this calls for considerable policy initiative.

There is an in-depth analysis of the retrospects and prospects of the financial sector. We have a detailed study of the reforms in regulation of the financial sector that are imperative, the basic purpose of the financial system, the legitimate expectations of common people, development orientation and finance as a supplement to macroeconomic management including capital account management and possibly in supporting large borrowing programmes of some governments.

Public policy, challenges and responsibility are the subjects discussed next. Reddy advocates the Tobin Tax as it has immense potential when used with complementary policies, especially counter-cyclical and macro prudential measures. Tax regime should cover all instruments and markets, including derivatives. Managing fiscal consequences at the national level is constraining increased globalisation of finance. There is need for a recalibration of globalised finance.

Dr Reddy concentrates on the debates concerning global financial architecture and analyses the international monetary system. The recent crisis in Greece and the inability of the Euro to withstand shocks have led to belief in the merit for global autonomy in promoting SDR—based on a multi-polar monetary system wherein the Euro can emerge as a critical component. There is a succinct analysis of G20 framework, volatility in capital flows and the new global financial architecture. India's performance and prospects are dealt with in the concluding section.

Jagdish Bhagwati has rightly described the volume to be "a masterly book, to be read and savoured. A *tour de force*."

•

Windows of Opportunity: Memoirs of an Economic Adviser
by K.S. Krishnaswamy
Published by Orient Blackswan;
Pages 190; Price ₹ 440

The book under review is the memoirs of Dr K.S. Krishnaswamy, who is one of the most distinguished intellectuals of post-freedom India and has donned several hats with distinction. He began his career as a Lecturer in Bombay University, followed by two terms as Member of the Planning Commission and then by the Directorship of Economic Development Institute of the World Bank. Finally, he became the Executive Director and Deputy Governor of the RBI.

Dr Krishnaswamy bagged a Government of India (GoI) scholarship to the LSE in order to conduct research on 'Variation in Relative Shares of Productive Factors in National Income'. Prior to joining the LSE, he was introduced to Sachin Chaudhuri, who had started a new journal—*The Economic Weekly* (*EW*)—which went on to become the *Economic and Political Weekly* and attained a position of great influence. Krishnaswamy was the London correspondent of EW and his relationship with this periodical endured.

His first arena was the Planning Commission set up in 1950 to prepare plans for the country's economic development. According to a popular story: "There is a vacant chair at every cabinet meeting of Jawaharlal Nehru. It is reserved for the ghost of Prof Harold Laski." This famous statement brings out clearly the paramount influence on Indian administration of the LSE. Three important members were J.J. Anjaria, K.N. Raj and K.S. Krishnaswamy—all from LSE. The chapter on the first Planning Commission offers a vivid portrait of the first Prime Minister, Jawaharlal Nehru, who dominated the scene and literally drove everybody—the government, his party and the Planning Commission.

Krishnaswamy joined RBI as a senior research officer. His Annual Report for 1951-52 presented the Bank's assessment of the overall economic situation and the extent to which monetary policies could be adjusted in support of development finance, provided the government was ready to take the supply-side measures so as to allay price rises. He was closely connected with the A.D. Shroff Committee on finance for industry.

Krishnaswamy was deputed for two years to the Economic Development Institute of the World Bank in Washington, where he conducted seminars on national income analysis, monetary questions, development issues and some micro-analysis.

J.J. Anjaria who was Economic Adviser, recommended that Krishnaswamy should head a new division on economic policy and growth in the Planning Commission. This was his second stint with the Planning Commission. The years 1961-62 witnessed China's invasion of India, and Nehru's decline both physically and mentally. As Chairman, Nehru pleaded for "defence with development."

The World Bank sent a mission under Bernard Bell to review the prospects of Indian economy and the kind of foreign aid required. The mission dealt with sensitive issues and Bell quickly found out that he was not entirely welcome in Yojana Bhavan.

> When Bell said that he spoke with the authority of the World Bank President, Dr I.G. Patel told him severely that he spoke with the authority of the Indian Government and closed the meeting.

The year 1966 was an exceedingly difficult year. Increased spending by the government for defence plus development, together with crop failures and reduced foreign exchange available for food or raw material imports had pushed up domestic prices. The Bell Mission recommended devaluation of the Indian rupee. Krishnaswamy declared to his Deputy Chairman that he "saw no benefit in devaluation." Asoka Mehta said nothing. In the event, Krishnaswamy was left out of the discussions with the IMF on devaluation. With complete honesty Krishnaswamy writes:

> Perhaps I should have had the courage to walk out at that point....I just did not have the courage to say "so be it", a decision which has shamed me no end. The decision to devalue had been decided even before the team left for discussions with the Fund.

The author returned to RBI as Principal Adviser in 1972. By the 1970s, relations between the RBI and Central Government had changed enough to deny the former much of the prestige and independence deserved as an arbiter of the country's monetary policy. In a couple of years, Krishnaswamy had become Executive Director of the RBI. During the abominable Emergency, K.R. Puri was appointed as Governor and J.C. Luther as an Executive Director. Both were believed to be close to Sanjay Gandhi and ensured that the banking industry was turned into a handmaiden of the political bosses.

The intrusion of politics into banking became wider after the declaration of Emergency. Financial institutions had become extension of the PMO or even worse of Indira Gandhi's close advisers. Krishnaswamy rejected the application of the Central Bank of India for an additional loan of ₹ 25-30 lakh to the Maruti automobile company. Puri was told by the PMO that the loan must be sanctioned, by promptly raising the CAS (Credit Authorisation Scheme) limit. This he did without informing Krishnaswamy and the Department of Banking Operations and Development (DBOD).

The advent of the Janata government saw the exit of Puri and Luther. Until the new incumbent Dr I.G. Patel could take over, an interim Governor was sent from Delhi and that was M. Narasimham. Perhaps the only bitterness of this delightful memoir is in connection with M. Narasimham. The author is very frank about his erstwhile colleague in RBI. He writes very brutally:

> When Puri was removed and a temporary vacancy was to be filled, neither Hazari nor I was considered. ....These denials of important positions hurt me deeply... By the time I became Deputy Governor, Narasimham had taken over as the Banking Department Secretary and his minions became more interfering. Narasimham's attitude towards me had always been one of subdued hostility.

This memoir is inordinately brief, exceedingly well-written, truly candid and will be useful to all those interested in the functioning of the RBI and the Planning Commission; it also offers a bird's eye view of the history of Indian banking from 1950s to the present.

•

Monetary Policy in a Globalized Economy by Rakesh Mohan
Published by Oxford University Press;
Pages 348; Price ₹ 795

Dr Rakesh Mohan was twice Deputy Governor of the RBI. He was earlier Secretary, Department of Economic Affairs, Ministry of Finance, Director and Chief of Indian Council for Research on International Economic Relations (ICRIER) and Vice-Chairman, Infrastructure Development Finance Company (IDFC). He has also been Adviser to the Finance Minister, Director General of National Council of Applied Economic Research (NCAER). Most recently, he chaired the Committee on Financial Sector Assessment for India and the BIS Working Group on capital flows to emerging market economies (EMEs). As Deputy Governor, he has looked after the Monetary Policy Department, Department of Economic Analysis and Policy, and Financial Markets Department. After his academic pursuits at Imperial College London (in electric engineering), Yale and Princeton (economics), he had a fruitful stint at the World Bank before returning to India. According to S.S. Tarapore, an erstwhile Deputy Governor, Rakesh Mohan's,

> ..knowledge and analysis of macroeconomic issues as also monetary economics is nonpareil. He had an open mind on key policy issues. Starting with first principles, he used empirical evidence and practical knowledge of central banking operations to come out with novel and sound central banking policies.

His appointment as Distinguished Consulting Professor at the Stanford Centre for International Development at Stanford University is not only an honour for him, but also for the RBI.

Over the last two decades, the RBI has played a key role in propelling the Indian economy onto the world stage. Dr Rakesh Mohan lucidly and convincingly explains how this was done—the monetary policy and financial structure choices were made and the challenges that face the nation. He provides an invaluable guide to a complex subject which is of great relevance to policymakers, private sector and students. He covers a great deal of technical ground in a comprehensible manner, while tackling tough problems that have been at the heart of the situation of last two decades, Indian experience in the transition of its financial sector and conduct of monetary policy from a regime of extreme financial repression to that of an increasingly market-based system stands out in the global economy. There has been a distinct decline of inflation and related expectations and acceleration of growth in an environment of macroeconomic and financial stability. This period has been noted for financial deepening, efficiency and productivity gains in the domestic banking system, and growing depth and width of the domestic financial markets.

The book under review represents a collection of Rakesh Mohan's lectures and papers and reflect his thinking as it has evolved since 2002. He analyses the changes in the financial sector during the 1980s and 1990s which were noted for a large number of banking and financial sector crises, covering about 100 countries, both developed and developing, with the latest crisis enveloping the largest advanced economies. The advent of floating exchange rates, free trade flows, and cross-border capital flows, in the backdrop of growing deregulation and liberalisation, contributed to the financial instability during the 1980s and 1990s, as well as in the present decade. He covers areas as diverse as the evolution of central banking in India, the growth of industrial financing, reforms in banking, agricultural credit and several interesting global contradictions in monetary policy.

One distinguishing feature of the Indian economy has been that financial stability has been maintained successfully despite repeated shocks, both international and domestic. The underlying theme of the articles is that monetary policy and financial sector reform have been conducted in the context of increasing globalisation, while fostering growth and maintaining price and financial stability in India.

The first set of chapters deal with banking and finance and explain how the Indian financial sector has been bank-based and the funding of a substantial part of the economic activity has been dependent on efficient functioning of the banking system. The chapter,

'Transforming Indian Banking' discusses important policy issues that were confronting the financial sector, with ramifications for economic growth and for sustained profitability of the banking industry.

Another chapter deals with the unique role of the RBI in promoting agricultural credit—which it was bound to under the RBI Act. The chapter 'Agricultural Credit in India' spells out the fact that though the overall flow of institutional credit has increased over the years, there are still several gaps, inadequate provision of credit to small and marginal farmers, paucity of medium- and long-term lending and deposit mobilisation, heavy dependence on borrowed funds by major agricultural purveyors, and existence of an antiquated legal framework that hamper credit flows.

In an important article the author discusses ownership and governance in private sector, which explains the analytical foundations that underlie the RBI policy, leading to the strengthening of the Indian banking system and moving them towards international best practices through a consultative process. The objective of the banking sector reforms initiated in the early 1990s was to promote a diversified, efficient and competitive financial system that helped improve the allocational efficiency of resources. All these are cogently discussed in the chapter on 'Reforms, Productivity and Efficiency in Banking: The Indian Experience'.

The second half of the book deals with monetary policy and banking. The chapter 'Financial Sector Reforms and Monetary Policy' is a review of the experience since the early 1990s and forms a backdrop to discussion of the different aspects of monetary policy. A contemporary issue in central banking is the appropriate response of monetary policy to sharp asset price movements. Monetary policy has emphasised the need to be watchful about indication of rising aggregate demand embedded in consumer and business confidence, the growth of reserve money and money supply, the rising trade and current account deficits and also the quality of credit growth. The overall objective continues to be the maintenance of economic growth and financial stability. Monetary policy is increasingly required to take into account both domestic developments and those made in the global economy and global financial markets. All these find a place in the chapter on 'Challenges to Monetary Policy in a Globalizing World'. Rakesh Mohan explores some of the puzzles for contemporary monetary policy. A very interesting chapter is on the evolution of central banking in India. A great degree of variation is observed in the practice of monetary policy and central banking, both over time and across countries. While tackling the problem of liquidity, the author has expatiated on how the policy involved careful calibration taking into account diverse objectives of central banking, changes in the monetary policy framework and widening the set of instruments for liquidity management. The concluding chapter of the book 'Monetary and Financial Policy Responses to Global Imbalances' focuses on the issue of global imbalances that has been a subject of keen debate. Any action for orderly medium-term resolution of global imbalances is a shared responsibility and will bring greater benefit to all members and the international community than actions taken individually.

The volume bears the stamp of Mohan's scholarship and deep understanding of working of the monetary and financial system. It is compulsory reading for all students of banking, finance and management. The book has 72 tables, 33 figures, 9 boxes and 2 annexures, which furnish invaluable information in a nutshell.

Mention must be made of the author's modesty when he declares that ".. although the book bears my name as the author, it really encompasses the collective work of the highly dedicated Reserve Bank staff." He pays rich tribute to Usha Thorat and Shyamala Gopinath, two current Deputy Governors, for inducting him very skillfully and patiently into the art of liquidity management.

•

Growth with Financial Stability: Central Banking in an Emerging Market by Rakesh Mohan

Published by Oxford University Press;
Pages 500; Price ₹ 950

The author of the book under review, Dr Rakesh Mohan was the Deputy Governor of the RBI twice and is presently the Professor of International Economics of Finance, School of Management, and Senior Fellow, Jackson Institute of Global Affairs, Yale University. He is also Senior Research Fellow of Stanford University. We had reviewed his earlier book, *Monetary Policy in a Globalized Economy*.

More than 100 countries—advanced, emerging, and developing alike—have suffered from financial crisis over the past 30 years. India is among the few which have not. That was the motivation for this book which provides an understanding of Indian macroeconomic, fiscal, monetary and financial policies as they have evolved over the years, and as they have contributed to the achievement of economic growth with financial stability.

The book analyses the record of Indian economic growth since 1947; proceeds to deal with financial sector reforms; and analyses monetary policy. We have an interpretation of the reasons for the global financial crisis and how it was contained in India. Critical reforms that are needed in other areas are also studied succinctly. Dr Rakesh Mohan believes that the key to maintaining and accelerating economic growth is a reform of overall government functioning. He argues that RBI must be allowed to continue its practice of consistent and harmonious blending of monetary policy with prudential regulation.

Monetary policy and financial sector reforms acquired paramount importance in our country in the background of the global financial crisis. The present book makes a sterling contribution on this vital topic. The author was a part of the policy group that dealt with this problem during a crucial period in the last decade. He had submitted a number of papers at different fora and has now revised and updated some of these. There are 12 essays in the book. The volume starts with a critical analysis of India's growth since Independence, when public sector was the engine of growth, fiscal policy stood for high levels of taxation so as to generate finance for investment in that sector and budget deficits were monetised to fund investments.

While it is undeniable that the RBI armoury was not well furnished, measures were taken to employ instruments like the Statutory Liquidity Ratio (SLR) and Cash Reserve Ratio (CRR) to stem excessive undue expansion of money supply. The country averted high levels of inflation which plagued several developing economies. Post-liberalisation, the financial sector reforms have served to enhance not just the competitiveness and efficiency of banks, but also ensured their stability. The RBI compelled banks to follow internationally acceptable prudential norms of capital adequacy, while accepting risk weighting of their assets and provisioning requirements. This resulted in credit being extended towards sound investments and abjuring speculative transactions. Indian banks were unaffected by the global turbulence during the East Asian financial crisis and the North Atlantic countries' financial meltdown.

With the practice of automatic monetisation of the central government's deficits getting phased out in the early 1990s, the RBI's ability to use monetary instruments was greatly strengthened. The Fiscal Responsibility and Budget Management Act guaranteed a substantial reduction in fiscal deficit at the central and state levels. The private sector garnered more resources from the market and the interest rates dropped significantly during 2003-2008. Since 2009, there has been a reversal.

Safeguarding financial markets against volatility has acquired paramount importance in managing exchange rate and foreign capital inflow. A gradualist approach was adopted in respect of capital account. While risk capital was permitted to flow liberally in the form of FDI and portfolio investments, short-term commercial borrowings were afforded only a limited scope. The impact of foreign capital volatility on portfolio investments was tempered through open market operations and 'sterilisation' measures.

The author presents a strong, well-constructed defence of the monetary policy pursued by the RBI over the past two decades. Unlike the central banks of many other countries which focused exclusively on controlling inflation, the RBI targeted price stability, exchange rate management and financial stability, coupled with adequate credit supply to sustain growth. RBI has maintained price stability and developed a sound financial sector, and without a shred of doubt has been successful in achieving financial stability. However recently, inflation has raised its ugly head and reached two-digit level, in spite of the RBI altering policy rates a dozen times in about 18 months. The economist points out that the financial system has failed in providing adequate credit to the farm sector and the small and micro enterprises. The development strategy should focus much more on agriculture, urban infrastructure, and human resource to maintain a substantial growth rate.

We have a masterly review of the post-1991 monetary and financial policies by one who played a major role in policy formulation. The book is strongly commended to all students of economics, banking, planning as well as the mandarins in Delhi.

•

Financial Policies and Everyday Life by S.S. Tarapore
Published by Academic Foundation;
Pages 334; Price ₹ 795

Shri S.S. Tarapore was the distinguished Deputy Governor of RBI and had served there for 35 years. He was seconded to the IMF from 1971-1979 and was the Chairman of several committees. He is presently connected with the Administrative Staff College of India and the Skoch Development Foundation.

The book under review–his articles from financial dailies--is a running commentary of India's recent financial policies and raises issues affecting the policymakers and participants in financial markets. It is divided into a dozen parts with 84 short chapters. The distinguishing quality of the volume is that no essay is longer than five pages and each essay tackles a subject of relevance with unusual simplicity, impressive quality and great authority. The subjects covered are macroeconomic perspectives, monetary-fiscal policies, external sector policies, exchange rate management and finally gold.

According to Tarapore, India cannot afford to experiment with adventurist macroeconomic policies in the belief that mild measures combined with questionable financial engineering would enable an economy to undertake the required adjustment, without too heavy a burden. He advocates early and strong measures in dealing with output and inflation cycles.

He strikes a strident note of warning that for a country like India which suffers from a 'savings' shortage, using created money to stimulate investment is bound to generate inflation that would take firm root in the economy. A sound macroeconomic policy will comprise fiscal rectitude, transparent approach to inflation, co-ordinated monetary fiscal policies and continuation of economic reforms. The author favoured greater sensitivity towards equity in direct taxes. In the context of setting up the Financial Sector Legislative Reforms Committee, he is for legislative measures to provide a degree instrument independence for RBI. Industrial houses must be allowed to set up new private sector banks. He has great faith in 'Gold' and has advocated preference of individuals for gold, stating it as "one of the wisest investment decisions." Gold has become a major international reserve asset and Dr Subbarao's decision to buy 200 tonnes of gold "would go down in history as his contribution to the RBI."

The first part of the book deals with "Macroeconomic Issues and the Global Crisis" and has six chapters. The author argues that Indian economy does not reflect a glut in savings related to investment opportunities and therefore the Keynesian remedy of pump-priming is inappropriate. What we need is a Hayekian slump where there is over-investment relative to savings.

Part II of the book is on "Monetary Policy and the Global Crises" and has 10 articles. The finely balanced policy of the RBI and its statesman-like maturity and judgement, which met the imperatives of the day without jeopardising stability comes in for praise.

The third part of the book is on the "Need for Monetary Tightening" and has nine articles. The section has lot of stern and strong advice for RBI as to how to fight inflation. Part IV—"Clawing back to Monetary Easing"—has 10 articles connected with the period 2010-11. Tarapore is all praise for RBI for its policies of deregulation of savings bank deposit rate. "Fiscal Policy and Distributive Justice" is the subject of the next part with twelve articles. Dealing with general subjects, Tarapore calls for setting up of a National Commission which should submit periodic reports on inflation and inflationary expectations. There are interesting articles on direct taxes and budgets. Part VI on "Financial Stability"—five articles—asserts that Indian financial system remains robust and well-equipped in order to face the headwinds of instability. A crucial subject, "Financial Legislative Reforms" forms the subject of Part VII. In four of the chapters, the author argues that RBI should seek the government's approval only on matters regarding which the legislation mandates that government approval is necessary. The RBI ought to articulate the need for changes in the Act. A landmark is the setting up of the Financial Sector Reforms Commission. It has an important role to play in banking. Three articles are devoted to this issue.

Other four parts deal with bank mergers, private banks, industrial houses, SB (savings bank) rates de-regulation, know your customer (KYC) process, mutual funds, exchange rate management, forex regulations for individuals and gold. The last part is on Dr Y.V. Reddy, Dr Rakesh Mohan and the Mohanty Working Group.

This is a valuable collection of brilliant and clear analysis of our country's financial policies. It is very useful for the bankers, planners, economists and students of banking and public policy.

•

**Interpreting Financial Policies for the Common Person
by S.S. Tarapore**
Published by LexisNexis;
Pages 191; Price ₹ 245

Harry Truman, an American President, proclaimed, "Give me a One-handed Economist. My Economic Advisers advocate one set of policies arguing 'on the one hand' and strongly espouse exactly opposite set of policies arguing 'on the other hand'." Economists are generally exemplary obfuscators. But there are splendid exceptions. S.S. Tarapore is one. He is a distinguished member of the RBI family, retiring as Deputy Governor. Clear thinking is his hallmark and precise writing is his passport. Eloquent proof is available in the book under review.

The book is for the *aam aadmi* who has not specialised in finance and economics, but is keen to know what makes the economy tick. The author believes that the common person should have a working knowledge of the nature and significance of financial policies. The lay citizen must not be trampled by the juggernaut of jargon. So Tarapore explains important concepts and terms in simple easy-to-comprehend language.

The book's origin is the "Syndicated Column" which reached out to the common man on issues relating to finance and appeared in four languages in as many papers. The book has 52 chapters divided into eight parts, each being centered on a policy. None of the essays is longer than three pages and there is no 'strain' to the brain. Only 'gain'.

The first part is devoted to overall issues. Ignoring the social tensions resulting from excessive inflation would be dangerous for India. We have paid the price of paying undue attention to the global situation, which caused India to end up with the highest inflation rates among the EMEs. It is imperative for increased employment to be at the top of the policy agenda and we must achieve a quantum leap in employment. While there is a need to step up agricultural output, as a large proportion of the people still lives off agriculture, it is recognised that future development of agriculture will be water-centric. The author dreads the impact of the current drought that occurred in 2013 in some parts of Maharashtra. He argues that depositors cannot expect higher deposit rates and for financial assets to compete with gold. It is essential to have inflation-indexed instruments with principal and interest indexed to inflation.

The second part is dedicated to monetary policy. Tarapore supports monetary tightening by RBI and urges it to resist pressures from the government in order to lower interest rates and create liquidity. His advice to depositors is to lock funds in 2-3 years maturities. They should prefer Gold Exchange Traded Funds or Gold Fund of Funds.

Part III dwells on control of the savings bank deposit rate. Tarapore is convinced that the banks have cartelised the rates and should be subject to examination by the Competitive Commission of India. The cartel should be broken in the interest of the common person.

Select banking issues affecting laymen form the subject of the next part. Tarapore opines that *vis-à-vis* financial inclusion and financial literacy, greater emphasis must be laid on the quality of services than on ambitious numerical targets. Financial literacy is a noble social cause. The Damodaran Committee Report on Customer Service is analysed. The bulk of the customers, according to the author, need traditional banking services. A very touching essay is on the trauma caused by the death of a bank customer. The immediate family were left without access to their own funds. Owing to the author's advocacy, the problem has been alleviated. He is for the post office emerging as a full-fledged bank.

Part V covers fiscal issues. The author recommends reduction in iniquities of the direct tax system. The LPG (liquefied petroleum gas) subsidy problem has been thoroughly dissected. External sector issues are tackled in the next part. Tarapore traces the evolution of the non-resident deposit schemes, and analyses the BoP current account deficit which had become a full-blown problem by March 2013.

Gold is the subject of the next part and the author cautions that gold should not be more than 5-10 per cent of an individual investor's portfolio. Tarapore advocates a Gold Bank, proposal for which has won approval from a RBI Working Group. Certain other issues are discussed including NBFCs (non-banking financial companies) Report. The author is convinced that the Financial Sector Legislative Reforms Committee has been cavalier in the treatment of financial inclusion.

This is a book to cherish as it is distinguished by clarity of thought, felicity of expression and ease in communication. It is warmly commended to all common people, students of banking, bankers and planners.

•

Perspectives On Development: Memories of a Development Economist by V.V.Bhatt
Published by Academic Foundation;
Pages 135; Price ₹ 595

Shri M. Narasimham, ex-Governor of RBI, in his gracefully written reminiscences *From Reserve Bank To Finance Ministry and Beyond* recalls the halcyon days of the Research Department of the RBI and the celebrated 'Gang of Four' which included M. Narasimham, V.V. Bhatt, A.G. Chandavarkar and D.R. Khatkhate. These "Four Musketeers" rose to phenomenal heights occupying exalted positions in the world of banking, development and academia. M. Narasimham wrote of Dr V.V. Bhatt:

> ...A soft-spoken person, an erudite scholar. And apart from being a first-rate economist, he had deep interests in philosophy. He could discuss, with equal felicity, capital coefficients and the subtler nuances of the verses of the Bhagavad Gita.

The book under review is the memoirs of a development economist of international repute, who began his career as a lecturer in S.L.D. Arts College at Ahmedabad. He joined the RBI Research Department in 1953 and continued till 1972, rising to the level of Adviser. Later on, he became Chief Executive of the Industrial Development Bank of India (IDBI) and from there ascended to the post of the Chief of the Public Finance Division of the World Bank. Dr Bhatt was offered the post of Deputy Governor in RBI, but had turned it down because of a heart attack in 1980.

As a young student, Bhatt took part in Satyagraha organised by Gandhiji and was jailed for two months in the Sabarmati Jail. He learnt economics in the distinguished Bombay School of Economics which had a galaxy of illustrious teachers and equally illustrious students. Along with Bhatt studied Dharma Kumar, later Editor of the *Cambridge Economic History of India* and Shri Nadkarni who became Chairman of the State Bank of India. Shri Bhatt had secured First Class First, bagged the K.T. Telang Gold Medal and the William Wederburn scholarship. Against the trend of running to Oxford or Cambridge or LSE, Bhatt chose to study at Harvard and what a list of distinguished professors who taught him—Schumpeter, Leontief, Hansen, Haberler, Gerschenkron, Dussenbury and Carl Keysen. He obtained his Doctorate on 'Choice of technology and techniques in India and developing countries'.

Dr V.V. Bhatt joined RBI and served for almost 20 years. Governor C.D. Deshmukh—visionary that he was—started strengthening the Department of Research by recruiting young and promising economists. At that time in RBI, there were outstanding economists like J.V. Joshi (a star pupil of J.M. Keynes) and Dr B.K. Madan. The Research Department was one of the most creative and effective departments, even amongst other central banks of the developing and even developed countries. It collected, analysed and published data in its Reports on Currency and Finance, Annual Reports and Trend and Progress in Banking. The Department was also actively involved in improving the database for planning. It undertook several studies regarding estimates of savings and investment, patterns of income distribution, money supply analysis, non-inflationary level of deficit financing, and impact of PL 480 funds on money supply. All these studies were published in the monthly bulletins of the RBI.

The author started contributing several seminal articles on development to distinguished journals like Economic Journal, Oxford *Bulletin of Statistics* and *Economia Internationale*. Most of these articles were published in a book, *Employment and Capital Formation in Underdeveloped Economies*. Dr Hannan Ezekiel, who was an economist with the IMF wrote about this book—"All the elements of development strategy of the second Five Year Plan were anticipated in the work done by Dr Bhatt in 1951-52."

Dr Bhatt and his peers contributed in a significant manner to the *Economic Weekly* founded by Sachin Chaudhari. This weekly had later become the *Economic and Political Weekly*, which flourished under the intellectual giant Krishna Raj and is held in great respect in the intellectual world.

At a seminar for young economists arranged by the International Economic Association and the Bombay School of Economics, several distinguished economists from all over the world took part—Joan Robinson, Nicholas Kaldor, Tarshis, Downie and others. Robinson and Kaldor paid a visit to the RBI and conveyed to Governor Rama Rau their deep appreciation of the contribution of Dr Bhatt and hailed him as a star participant.

Mention must be made of the heated discussions on the impact of PL 480 assistance on money supply. While B.R. Shenoy argued that it would stoke the inflationary fires, Bhatt and Khatkhate vehemently countered this, stating that it was widely accepted to be not inflationary.

Dr Bhatt describes his experience as an RBI nominee director on the boards of public sector banks. He refused to agree to conditions that he should liaise with the government director and took an independent stand on all items for discussion on the basis of what he considered right. He was fiercely independent.

For three years, Dr Bhatt was the Chief Executive of IDBI and here he laid the foundation for evolving criterion for evaluation of capital projects. During his term, he was deputed to Economic Commission for Asia and the Far East (ECAFE) as a consultant and reviewed critically India's performance during the first two decades. This is published in a book entitled *Two Decades of Development: The Indian Experience*.

Dr Bhatt had a stint during 1964-65 at the Asian Institute of Economic Development (AIED), where he conducted seminars on the theories of economic development, critical variables for initiating economic development, planning process and international aspects of development. These were published in a book—*Some aspects of Development Strategy*. Dr Bhatt used this book as a text when he was an adjunct professor at the American university in Washington, teaching economic development. Along with Nasir Ahmed Kahn, Dr Bhatt prepared a monograph, *A Framework for Economic Development of the Lower Mekong Countries*, which was published by the Institute and ECAFE.

In September 1972, Dr Bhatt joined the Economic Development Institute of the World Bank. The institution trained government officials from developing countries, educating them on development economics. Dr Bhatt's proposal for an Asian Association of Development Banks was accepted. The World Bank appointed him as Chief of the Public Finance Division of its Economics Department. In this capacity, he promoted two research projects—one on financial structures and policies for development and the other on management of public enterprises. These related to Philippines, Mexico, and Brazil. Informal credit markets were also studied in respect of India and South Korea.

During the decade ending 2000, the author served as an independent consultant to the World Bank. He prepared studies on countries such as Yemen, Ghana, Japan, Sri Lanka, etc.

It is a matter of great pride that all studies undertaken by the author have been used at Harvard Business School and management institutes in India.

A final chapter of the book presents a theme beloved to the author and reveals profound insights into the development literature since Adam Smith. Admirable summaries are furnished of the theories of Schumpeter, Marx and Gerschenkron.

Dr Bhatt is a star performer in the collection of world development economists and his work had a major impact on planning and development process. The memoirs recreate the events in the formative period of India's development process. The poet Wordsworth sang—

> Bliss it was in that dawn to be alive
>
> But to be young was very heaven.

How true is this to the band of economists like Dr Bhatt and his ilk who were young when our development process was in its nascent stage!

This is a memoir of great worth and is compulsory reading for all development economists and students of Indian economic history.

•

A Better India, A Better World by N.R. Narayana Murthy
Published by Penguin;
Pages 290; Price ₹ 499

N.R. Narayana Murthy is the man behind one of the biggest IT (information technology) ventures in India. He is the Founder-Chairman of Infosys Technologies Limited, a global software consulting company. To gauge the strength of Infosys, we recall his words, "We are a company with fifty thousand people, we operate in thirty eight countries; and we have people of forty-five nationalities."

He serves on the boards of Unilever, HSBC, NDTV, Ford Foundation and the UN Foundation. He also serves on the boards of Cornell University, Wharton School, Singapore Management University, Indian Institute of Information Technology, and INSEAD. He is a living legend and an exemplary leader. His life has proved that honesty, transparency and moral integrity can co-exist with business acumen. *The Economist* (London) ranked Narayana Murthy among the most-admired global leaders in 2005. He topped the *Economic Times* list of India's most powerful CEOs for three consecutive years—2004 to 2006. He has been awarded the Padma Vibhushan by the GoI, the Legion d'Honneur by the Government of France, and the CBE by the British government.

Narayana Murthy has proved that it is possible to benchmark with the global best from India. Our earlier Prime Minister, Shri Vajpayee is reported to have stated that earlier, foreigners would visit India to see the Taj Mahal and a few temples. Today they have begun asking for software engineers from India. Infosys has a paramount role in making this happen. There has been a sea-change in attitude towards business after success of Infosys. Businessmen are even being invited to join the Prime Minister's Advisory Council.

The author says it is extremely important not only to have a great idea, but also to ensure that all efforts are invested so that the idea is executed in the right manner. Business must be pursued legally and ethically. Entrepreneurs must make sure that the value system is adhered to by them and they must live by the principle that the softest pillow is a clear conscience. Narayana Murthy believes in creating an environment of openness, discussion, debate, pluralism and meritocracy.

While India is the world's largest democracy, about 300 million Indians are still prey to hunger, illiteracy and disease, and 53 per cent of India's children are still undernourished. So the author asks some pertinent questions. What will it take for India to overcome poverty? When will the fruits of development reach the poorest of the poor, and wipe the tears from the eyes of every man, woman and child, as Mahatma Gandhi had dreamt? And how should this, our greatest challenge ever, be negotiated? All these questions and more are answered by Narayana Murthy in this testament. In this extraordinarily inspiring and visionary book, N.R. Narayana Murthy, who pioneered, designed and executed the Global Delivery Model that has become the cornerstone of India's success in IT services outsourcing, shows us that a society working for the greatest welfare of a massive magnitude must focus on two simple things: values and good leadership. Drawing on the remarkable Infosys story and the lessons learnt from the two decades of post-reform India, Narayana Murthy lays down the ground rules that must be followed, if future generations are to inherit a truly progressive nation.

The book has 38 speeches, culled out of over 150 speeches that he has made over last few years, dealing with a variety of subjects, to audiences both in India and abroad. Subjects covered are students, values, national issues, education, leadership, corporate and public governance, corporate responsibility, philanthropy, entrepreneurship, globalisation and of course Infosys. It is a manifesto for the youth, the architects of the future, and a compelling argument for why a better India holds the key to a better world. He reveals his vision of a better life through innovative entrepreneurship. He is an avid believer of economic reforms and globalisation. According to him, the market should act as an arbiter and the government a facilitator.

As one reads the book under review, one is convinced of how the author achieved excellence through his basic decency and transparent honesty. Narayana Murthy's panacea for our poverty lies in entrepreneurship that results in job creation on a huge scale. His experience with Infosys is the sheet anchor of his credo.

He argues convincingly of the paramount role of corporates in contributing to eradication of poverty by ploughing a portion of the wealth they create. He gives a succinct analysis of the growth of Infosys with his firm conviction not to compromise on principles. The course of his life was changed by a meeting with a famous American computer engineer in 1968, when he was a graduate student in IIT Kanpur.

He discussed exciting developments in the field of computer science, explaining how they would alter our future. The student was hooked and hitched his bandwagon to the stars. It is a matter of surprise that in 1991, serious discussions were held to sell Infosys for a million dollars. He recalls the travails he bore patiently including delays by RBI (of which he later became a Central Board Director)—"the long waits of four to six hours to obtain part of our own hard-earned dollars to support my other six other founders." He ruefully recalls how he had to pledge the jewellery of Sudha Murthy in order to raise money for the maintenance of his six colleagues who were engaged in our project sites in foreign countries.

Narayana Murthy warmly supports transfer of farm labour on a large scale to manufacturing units so as to reduce our poverty level and quotes the success of China. He argues for role models in public life and believes in visionary leadership to solve our country's gargantuan problems. No better advice could be given than the last lines of the book:

> Be original, daring different and unreasonable. Work hard, have good values, put the interest of the country in every deed of yours and make this country the best place in the world.

•

Reinventing Development Economics: Explorations from the Indian Experiment by N.A. Mujumdar
Published by Academic Foundation;
Pages 268; Price ₹ 995

The most regrettable aspect of this book is that the author passed away two days before its release. Dr Mujumdar served in RBI for over three and a half decades. He had wide interests in rural issues, monetary and fiscal policies and international problems. He taught at Mumbai University and had the distinction of being awarded the prestigious Nuffield Fellowship at Oxford. On his return to India, he joined the RBI in 1960 as Research Officer, and retired as Principal Adviser, Department of Economic Analysis and Policy in 1988. His services were sought by the IMF for secondment to the central banks of five different countries—Zambia, Mauritius, Tanzania, Belize and Cambodia.

Dr Mujumdar was an authority on Agricultural Economics, and was until his demise the Editor of the Indian Journal of Agricultural Economics and the Honorary Professor at the Society for Development Studies. He is the author of a number of books including two volumes on Indian Agriculture. His last book was *India's New Development Agenda*.

The book under review is an attempt at exploring the new aspects of development philosophy. Divided into six broad sections, it addresses the issues of: growth and development, monetary policy, banking policy, fiscal policy, food security and global environment, with reference to the Indian economy. The main underlying theme of all the articles in the volume is promoting growth which is all-round and inclusive, equitable and above all growth which ultimately leads to the emergence of a value-based compassionate society.

In his introduction, Dr Mujumdar argues that we must grow up from conventional growth economics trapped in market theology to resonate to the larger concerns of holistic development including promotion of broad-based decentralised growth, which alone could facilitate access by the poor to employment, food, nutrition and health and quality education. Inclusive growth is imperative for sustainability.

India's development experience during the decades (1991-2011) provides good insights into the issue veering away from Milton Friedman to Mahatma Gandhi, away from food market theology towards building a value-based society.

The book has 54 articles and is divided into six broad sections. Section one is devoted to 'Growth and Development'. The first essay is on India's development drama during 1991-2011, during which many basic issues were overlooked leading to neglect of agriculture, disdain for subsidies and worrisome disregard for the elementary principles of food security. The author has divided the period into two phases: 1991-2004—the Milton Friedman phase characterised by ruthless seeking of higher growth rate with its attendant adverse effects on development issues. The second phase is the Gandhi phase, when our policymakers rediscovered Gandhi's development philosophy—community-centred development. There is a crying need for a value-based compassionate society. The article on World Development Reports proves that these were mainly summaries of inside and outside academic research and they offered no meaningful development policy guidelines. They were "empty vessels offering little meaningful development."

Dr Mujumdar has asserted that massive imports of gold threatened to erode the strength of our economy through their impact on household sector financial saving, on current account deficit and on the BoP. He has recommended imposition of quantitative ceiling on gold imports.

The second section is on 'Monetary Policy'. The comments of *The Economist*, London—"Judging by the numbers, RBI is among the world's best central bankers. RBI has more brains, muscle and integrity, relative to the best State Bodies." Thanks to the RBI, the nation could escape the Asian Currency Crisis of 1997 and the global financial crisis of 2008. Nobel Laureate Joseph Stiglitz declared—"The US financial system collapsed because we did not have a Reddy at the helm." The mandate of central banks extend beyond price stability and include bank regulation and supervision, thereby promoting growth.

Section III is devoted to 'Banking Policy'. Dr Mujumdar highlights that obsession with implementing Basel norms and internalising international best practices led to several policy distortions. This led the RBI to make a plea for focusing on India-specific issues. Indian banks should think global and act local. The author analyses the Report of the Committee on Customer Service headed by M. Damodaran and lauds the excellent recommendations.

The fourth section is devoted to fiscal policy. There is no continuity or consistency in the budget proposals because they are not informed by any economic philosophy and ad hocism is writ large on them.

Section V is on "Food Security". The emphasis ought to be on creating an environment which enables households to purchase foodgrains through employment generation, moderate open market prices of rice and wheat and streamline market arrangements of some items like fruits and vegetables.

The concluding section is on global environment. The Enron, World. Com and Xerox exposures have unveiled the darker side of western capitalism, where in the quest for short-term gains wrong doings are overlooked. The collapse of Andersen, one of the big five accounting firms has, in the wake of the Enron scandal, added a new dimension to systemic infirmities. The final article catalogues the lessons for central banks from the global financial crisis.

This is a seminal work of great use to bankers, politicians and planners, covering a wide ambit of subjects of crucial importance to the nation.

•

Growth and Finance: Essays in Honour of C. Rangarajan
Edited by Sameer Kochhar
Published by Academic Foundation;
Pages 351; Price ₹ 1095

The book under review is a Festschrift in honour of Dr C. Rangarajan There are 16 essays by 20 eminent authorities on banking, finance, management and public administration. In a preface the Home Minister Shri P. Chidambaram writes:

> Today, there is no one I know of who is more sought after, more often consulted, more dependable. more impartial ,more neutral ,and more valuable in the advice he gives as far as economic policy matters are concerned than Dr Rangarajan....I think it (this book) is a remarkable tribute not only to a very fine intellectual but also a very fine human being.

Several aspects of our daily lives that we take for granted today—for example ATMs, credit cards—are attributable to the financial reforms that Dr Rangarajan brought about as Governor of RBI.

In a foreword, Dr Manmohan Singh pays tribute to Dr Rangarajan. Dr Rangarajan has taught at Wharton School of Finance and Commerce, Graduate School of Business Administration in New York and IIM Ahmedabad. He was Member of the Planning Commission, Deputy Governor and later Governor of RBI, Governor of Andhra Pradesh, Chairman of the Twelfth Finance Commission and is presently Chairman of the Prime Minister's Economic Advisory Council. We have a pithy assessment of Dr Rangarajan by one of his successors Governor Subbarao, who has unarguably asserted:

> Dr Rangarajan..straddled both academia and the government. What makes him unique though is the way he constructively blended what are two disparate worlds. He brought deep scholarship over a range of academic disciplines to bear on public policy...He remained deeply sensitive to real life concerns. It is this unique trait that has set him apart as one of today's most credible thinkers and advisers. Fittingly, a critic labelled him as "philosopher king".

The 16 essays in this volume are essentially a labour of love, affection and admiration for Dr Rangarajan. The volume has a true head start with an unusual anecdotal history of the tumultuous times during 1982-1997 by Shri S.S. Tarapore, who rightly mourns that in India anecdotal history is neglected as senior officials generally do not maintain personal diaries. He has presented a fascinating account of how battles were fought, policies were fashioned out after heated debates and recounts the genesis of crucial decisions made during that period. Subjects tackled included BoP crisis of 1990-91, devaluation of rupee and JPC Committee. Tarapore brings out vividly how Dr Rangarajan encouraged those working under him to articulate views diametrically opposed to his own. According to Tarapore, "Generations to come will scarce believe that Plato's 'Philosopher King' walked the corridors of the Reserve Bank in flesh and blood." One devoutly wishes that Shri Tarapore writes the anecdotal history of the Reserve Bank during its first 75 years.

Dr Subbarao, the Governor of RBI, has analysed the ills that plague the banking system and how we should ensure that banking takes steps to evolve, grow and innovate in response to the developments in financial markets and institutions. The banking sector in India has four challenges to meet head on—deepening financial inclusion, financing infrastructure, strengthening risk management and improving efficiency. Facing these challenges is sure to make banking exciting.

The essay by Kanagasabhapathy and Radhakrishnan focuses on the mainstream views on transparency and autonomy in the formulation and conduct of monetary policy, including those out of the IMF Code. It calls for exploring the possibility of extending the management concept of 'Johari Window' to transparency in public policies with a particular reference to monetary policy.

John Massey emphasises the importance of financial services in developing growth, employment generation, capital allocation, savings, wealth distribution and risk management. Financial inclusion is the process of ensuring access to financial services and timely and adequate credit provision. The author has commended the efforts of RBI so as to increase financial literacy.

Shyamala Gopinath pays tribute to Dr Rangarajan, recalling her indebtedness to him. She recounts his role in steering the country out of the crisis in the early 1990s and laying down the foundation of the subsequent policy framework, which put the economy on a robust and resilient growth. Her essay on a macro-prudential approach to regulation reveals that many ideas were originated by Dr Rangarajan.

Other eminent writers are Y.V. Reddy, K.C. Chakravarty, Ravi Narain, Kirit Parekh and others. Due to space constraints, it is not possible to deal with all the essays in this volume, but reading this volume will adequately highlight the giant role played by Dr Rangarajan in several fields of Indian economy. The volume that has been brought out by the Skoch Group is edited by Sameer Kochhar, the Chairman. He is the President of Skoch Development Foundation which is our country's leader as the think tank on social and financial matters. We owe a deep debt to Sameer Kochhar and Academic Foundation for bringing out this valuable Festschrift by a number of authorities in several fields. No better tribute to Dr Rangarajan is possible. The book is warmly commended to all economists, bankers, administrators, planners and students of economics and banking.

Monetary Governance in Search of New Space by A.Vasudevan
Published by Academic Foundation;
Pages 127; Price ₹ 695

Dr Vasudevan is Adviser on monetary policy to the Central Bank of Nigeria. He has held exalted positions in IMF and had served in RBI in several capacities, including that of Executive Director. His book *Central Banking for Emerging Market Economies* is considered to be the Bible for central bankers. He is a prolific writer and imparted a new shape, colour and content to the earlier drab RBI publications, like the Monthly Bulletins and several other Reports.

The book under review tackles the problem regarding relevance of the role of money and banking, especially in the context of the global crisis that had hit the economic world like a tsunami. The author deals thoroughly with the challenges to governance of central banking ably, assisted by his deep experience and thorough theoretical mastery combined with expertise in public policy in India, Nigeria and other nations and international organisations.

In his Introduction, Governor of the Central Bank of Nigeria, Sanusi Lamido Sanusi writes:

> His vast wealth of knowledge garnered from his days as a central bank researcher-cum-academic in India and Adviser to the Executive Director for India at the IMF has been brought to bear in this veritable information book, in lucid style and with remarkable clarity of thinking.

Monetary governance deals with governance through sound economic policy, just as political governance deals with political aspects of society. It has national as well as international dimensions. They both interact in the globalised world of economic business as well as ideas.

The discussions in G20 led to the recognition of the idea of devising mechanisms that would bring out a standardised financial discipline worldwide. The Financial Stability Board recommended International Standards and Codes in 12 areas. These have been accepted by the G20 and the multi-lateral financial institutions. The events leading to the global financial and economic crisis, beginning in the middle of 2007, show that complacency together with the absence of thorough and regular monitoring of marketplace realities has been at the heart of the matter. The crisis opened a window of opportunity for the governments and central bankers to search for new space for policies and their implementation so as to promote national interests without jeopardising the interests of rest of the world.

This brief book has six chapters. The first chapter is devoted towards explaining the meaning of the term 'Monetary Governance'. It consists of international institutions and processes required for functioning of the tasks devolving on central banks and governments to achieve specific objectives. The second chapter deals with the institutional requirements, the institutional bodies that ensure growth, price stability and improved income and wealth and finally, distribution and promotion of human development. The architecture of monetary governance should ensure co-ordination of the actions undertaken by Governments and central banks. The next chapter's analysis is concerned with governments, and central banks and commercial banks, pension fund management entities, foreign exchange dealers and operators, mutual funds and other brokers. We have a cogent review of the functions of the Central Bank and the other players listed above. The economist calls for a thorough screening of all financial innovative products. The fourth chapter is dedicated to analytics and the international dimensions of monetary governance in detail from the point of view of emerging economies. What is imperative is good analytical framework for both fiscal and monetary authorities. The fifth chapter is about international dimension of the framework for global governance—to the extent that the major multi-lateral institutions represent the financial arm of international diplomacy— the IMF and the World Bank get involved. This is indicated by the high level of participation by Heads of States and Finance Ministers in G20 meetings. There is a succinct analysis of the IMF and the World Bank and their important committees. The Development Committee has 26 members and deals with issues of development and transfer of financial resources, trade and global environment issues.

Existing multi-lateral institutions and their operations, bye-laws and rules need to be reformed, and a number of issues have to be resolved. Industrially emerging economies have to be committed to ensure that the financial and economic imbalances do not recur. International institutions should co-ordinate their activities for the common good across countries. The final chapter emphasises that it has become imperative to make sure that both the domestic and international organisations, banks and other financial institutions are closely screened and regulated, along with the setting up of sound supervisory systems. Sound monetary governance, along with strong political commitment will act as a light at the end of the tunnel.

The volume is studded with copious references and is compulsory reading for all those connected with monetary policy and financial regulations, planners, economists, bankers and all students of banking.

•

Managing Risks in Commercial and Retail Banking
by Amalendu Ghosh
Published by John Wiley & Sons Inc.;
Pages 550; Price US $ 90

Shri Amalendu Ghosh was Chief of the Department of Banking Supervision of RBI, where he served for 36 years. He is an expert in supervision of banks, risk management and was closely connected with the implementation of the new Basel Capital Accord. He has brought out a manual for conduct of bank supervision, especially for the switch to risk-based bank supervision system. His rich experience as risk management consultant to two commercial banks has endowed the present volume with extraordinary authenticity and reliability. Ghosh is eminently qualified to write on risk management and the book under review is the quintessence of his experience. The book has been published by John Wiley, the oldest publisher in the US who is noted for their books on risk management, financial engineering, valuation and financial instruments analysis; and without doubt Ghosh's book is a valuable contribution.

The book is divided into seven parts that deal with risks management, approaches and systems, credit risk management, market risk management, operational risk management, risk-based internal audit, corporate governance and lessons learnt from the South-East Asian and American financial crises.

International banking world is governed by the new Basel Capital Accord of 2006 which is more risk-sensitive than the earlier accord of 1988. It has adopted a counter-party rating-based approach for regulatory capital assessment. A new concept of economic capital has been ushered in to take care of unusual losses arising from traumatic events. The new accord encourages banks to embrace new models for risks-rating and measurement. Supervisory authorities have taken new initiatives to reduce financial sector vulnerability. The book details new capital accord issues, including those specified in the 2010 Basel Committee response to the global financial crisis and deals with all important aspects of risk management.

In the first part, we have a thorough analysis of what constitutes risks (types of risks) and offers a model of how banks should manage the risk problem. Banks should formulate a risk management policy, keeping in view their resources, expertise, strengths and weaknesses.

The second part is devoted to portraying succinctly the multitude of credit risk management issues and presents models for rating and evaluating them. The author offers techniques to review credit portfolios as also rating-based loan pricing mechanism. The next part is concerned with risks springing from market management and helps one to identify all forms of market risks. It also offers solution to tackle various types of risks. To achieve a measure of success, banks have to take operational risks; this issue is covered in the fourth part of the book. It is a thorough analysis of major operational setbacks that severely affect banks' functioning and future. Banks should formulate special policies for mapping products and activities into appropriate business lines for the identification of operational risks.

Very germane to efficiency in banking is the successful and scientific internal audit procedure and the fifth part of the book is dedicated to this important aspect. The ways to compile risk profiles of bank branches are explained lucidly and the author expatiates clearly on how to initiate risk-focused audit and methods of writing risks-analytical reports. Banks' internal audit department should undertake an independent risk assessment of field offices and portfolios for focusing audit resources under the risk-based audit system.

Corporate governance is the subject matter of the sixth part. It is impressed on us how a sound and healthy risk management system protects the interests of the depositors, shareholders and debt holders. The Government and the Regulator should create an appropriate environment in order to enable banks to follow sound corporate governance practices.

The financial world was shaken up by the tsunamis of the South-East Asian and American financial crises. Giants tumbled like a pack of cards and confidence in the system received a rude shock. The last part of the book is a clinical analysis of these crises and the lessons we learnt; but more importantly, the steps banks ought to take to combat such occurrences.

This book brings together in an amazingly compact manner several items; such as basic concepts, methods and procedures in the field of risk management. The author's immense experience of bank supervision makes him go to the heart of each problem connected with risks and unerringly offers solutions. Each bank can evolve its own method of protecting its customers from risks. This book is a bible to all bankers, financial analysts, students of banking, accountants and auditors. It is a veritable treasure trove and contains the distilled experience of a seasoned banker and an authority on bank supervision.

•

Microfinance in India: Issues, Problems and Prospects:
A Critical Review of Literature by S.L. Shetty
Published by Academic Foundation;
Pages 658; Price ₹ 1295

It is an axiom in the world of Indian economics that any publication that has the imprimatur of *Economic and Political Weekly* is treated with great respect. The lead given by Sachin Chaudhury and his illustrious successor Dr Krishna Raj has invested all research products of *EPW* with high intrinsic value. The book under review is authored by Dr S.L. Shetty who was the first Director of the EPW Research Foundation. Prior to this, he was—for over a quarter century—a Senior Executive of the RBI, retiring as Adviser-in-charge of the Department of Research. He also served for four years in the Central Bank of Vanuvatu. He acquired a name for his pioneering study on 'Structural Retrogression in the Indian Economy' and he impressed all by his authoritative articles in *EPW* on subjects such as—monetary and fiscal policies and issues connected with development.

This study was originally funded by Hivos—an institution connected with the Netherland Humanist Movement. It was conceived as a review of the literature and a status report on microfinance (MF) during 2008; but in view of the sea-change since then, the Research Foundation decided to update and revise the study. MF is the sheet-anchor for poor citizens, especially women. Non-governmental organisations (NGOs) are the backbone of financial intermediation for the self-help groups (SHGs). Even with the strident official backing, their work has become an inalienable and invaluable part. Assisting the credit institutions has brought about an upsurge in the growth in microfinance institutions (MFIs). This growth led the RBI to appoint a Committee headed by Dr Malegam to recommend appropriate regulations for the sector. The Finance Ministry had formulated a Finance Bill proposing to confer regulatory powers on the RBI.

The book under review is a history of the development of MFIs and is an exhaustive analysis of the literature concerning the same. MF is one of the growing tools of development, and microcredit has become an integral part of social banking. The SHG-BL programme backed by NABARD is the largest MF programme in the world. There are a number of government programmes which support the poor.

The book is a comprehensive survey of the literature on MF movement in India and abroad. It offers a review of the performance of MFIs and answers the question whether MFIs can be a substitute for rural credit structure. In essence, the volume explores the challenges faced by MF institutions and the broader problems arising from serving the paramount needs of financial assistance to the poor.

The volume reviews steps taken by the authorities to close the gates in ground-level experiences, which oppose the policy of alleviating the distress of the poorer sections of the community. A number of significant suggestions have been made to strengthen and expand the role of MFIs.

The Editor admits at being aghast at the mind-boggling flurry of literature and financial press coverage on MF from myriad sources. The reader has been provided factual profiles of various microcredit programmes and their status in our country. We are apprised of the different regulatory measures and their impact. The often neglected limitations of the MF movement are studied in depth. There are a number of valuable suggestions to strengthen the movement.

The book has nine chapters. The first chapter sets the tone by a review of the concept of MF, its initial neglect in the studies conducted in economics and later emergence as an important sector in financial inclusion. The next chapter is devoted to the origin and history of the MF movement, models and the international initiatives taken in this field. While the world is aware of the Nobel Laureate Muhammad Yunus, the SEWA Bank run by women in Gujarat played a yeoman role as early as 1974. One of the chapters is dedicated to the experience in Bangladesh, Bolivia, Kenya, Nepal, Sri Lanka and Indonesia. The next two chapters are connected with the evolution of MF in India. There is a concise analysis of Sewa, SHG banks, NABARD, Sidbi and independent private institutions. The sixth chapter analyses the 2011 MF Bill in the background of the Report of the Malegam Committee and the response of RBI. The seventh and eighth chapters offer a succinct analysis of the evaluation and claims of outreach as well as critical assessment of the challenges faced by the MF movement. The final chapter is an assessment providing strong recommendations on financial system as the handmaid of growth and development.

This is a seminal volume of immense use to the students, planners and development experts. The book has a number of valuable tables, boxes, figures and an admirable 40 pages of references.

•

Microfinance for Macro Change Emerging Challenges
by Dr Deepali Pant Joshi
Published by Gyan Publishing House;
Pages 319; Price ₹ 750

The author of the book under review is an Executive of the RBI, a Fellow of Harvard University and is an authority on development economics.

Poverty reduction has been the main plank of the Indian planning process for over six decades, and access to finance by the poor and vulnerable group is undoubtedly an overriding factor. The aim of financial inclusion is to enlarge the role of the organised financial system so as to cover those segments with low incomes. Microfinance is a crucial motivator in this case and acts as a tool in improving productivity of the poor. This will spring from the evolution of a market serving the requirements of the poor.

Microfinance is the provision of a wide range of financial services, credit and insurance to the low income households and their micro enterprises. The poor can create projects that generate income and lift themselves up by their bootstraps. The SHG-Bank linkage programme is a laudable initiative to deliver financial services to the poor on a continuous basis. There has been a strident growth in this aspect and today the number of SHGs finance is over 30 lakhs. This programme confers gains on banks through externalisation of a part of the credit cycle. It ensures screening of borrowers, gauging credit requirements, appraisal and also enforcement of contracts.

The volume under review is an authoritative treatise on microfinancing, which surveys it at length, raises several questions and answers them with assurance. The first chapter furnishes a lucid background of how microfinance has become a paramount agent in poverty reduction. The next chapter deals with different delivery models assessing their success and drawbacks. NABARD sponsored SHG-Bank linkage programmes are dealt with in the next chapter. Chapter four highlights the role of regional rural banks (RRBs) and DCBs in delivery of microcredit to the poor. How microfinance has changed the life of women through SEWA along with examples of foreign experience, is the subject of the next chapter. Concrete examples from a number of developing countries regarding ways in which microfinance has strengthened the poor are provided in chapter six. The subsequent chapter reveals how the frontiers of conventional finance are being expanded. The concluding chapter tackles the challenges, issues and concerns.

The book is an admirable and succinct analysis of the gamut of microfinance dealing with objectives, participants, roles, and comparative advantages. The author has argued vehemently for expansion of the financial frontier to cover the remotest rural areas. This can be done by systematic mapping of financial services for the poor, improving knowledge industry, and co-ordinating at national and international levels.

The book has a bibliography and a number of tables detailing relevant parameters. Dr Rangarajan, former Governor of RBI has contributed a Foreword and declares that the book is a useful addition to the existing literature on the subject. The book is useful for planners, bankers, students of economics and those dedicated to alleviating poverty.

•

Politics Trumps Economics: The Interface of Economics and Politics in Contemporary India
Edited by Bimal Jalan and Pulapre Balakrishnan
Published by Rainlight/Rupa;
Pages 211; Price ₹ 500

The book under review is edited by two intellectuals. Dr Bimal Jalan was Governor of RBI and Member of the Rajya Sabha, each for six years. He held distinguished posts like Finance Secretary, Chairman of the Prime Minister's Economic Advisory Council. Prior to this, he served with distinction in the IMF and the World Bank. He is the author of several authoritative books.

The co-Editor Dr Balakrishnan was the recipient of the Malcolm Adiseshiah award for distinguished contribution to development studies. He is Professor in the prestigious Centre for Development Studies and a Senior Fellow in the Nehru Memorial Museum. He has two books to his credit.

India is the world's largest democracy and a rising economic power. This "revolution of rising expectations" has creaked to a halt and we are faced with a declining growth rate. A tsunami of corruption cases and poor implementation has led to stark despair enveloping the economy. What was rated to be a country of great expectations has been transformed into a nation sinking into the slough of despondency.

The editors ask a stark question—Why is this country which has a globally impressive talent pool languishing with the highest incidence of poverty in the world ? They set out to answer this crucial question by inviting 10 intellectuals to offer their analyses and answers. The book is divided into three sections—Politics, Governance and Policy. All the three are closely inter-related because politics determines governance and policymaking. Governance in turn determines outcomes, and successful policymaking has a great impact on the shape of politics.

According to the latest World Bank report on poverty, India accounts for one-third of the world poor or people living on less than ₹ 65 a day. The underlying cause is something other than mere economics slowing the pace of growth and poverty alleviation. It is the ever-present politics. Jalan highlights the importance of adapting economic policies to the evolving situation in terms of what the economy needs at any point of time. Since 1989, we have witnessed the emergence of Coalition Politics. India had nine governments in the past 23 years with an average life of less than two years and a half. A survey found that nearly 29 per cent of the candidates in the Lok Sabha had criminal antecedents. Corruption and scams have become common. There is a crying need to introduce radical political reforms so as to stamp out corruption. The power of the ubiquitous small parties to destabilise coalitions poses a grave danger. Jalan argues for tightening of anti-defection laws and ensuring courts give highest priority to the cases of elected leaders with criminal records.

Dipankar Gupta has lucidly recounted how politics trumps economics. The most energetic political expressions were the anti-corruption movement of 2011, the unrest in the aftermath of the brutal rape in December 2012 and the rise of Aam Aadmi Party (AAP) in 2012. Dividing voters along old fault lines was once as easy as parting one's hair but not any longer. The earlier line that separated a farmer from a worker is slowly getting erased. As a result, the unities between the citizens will be much more than seen in the past.

Pulapre Balakrishnan has tackled the problem of governance for facilitating an inclusive growth. We have to empower the poor economically. The poor have to be turned producers by equipping them adequately for the task and creating a market for their produce. Since governance is a political outcome, it is politics that will determine the range of inclusive growth.

Deepak Mohanty concentrates on monetary policy and ways to control inflation and ensure growth. We should have inclusive growth with stability. He analyses recent developments in monetary policy and its role in fostering financial stability. Monetary policy aims at price stability, growth and financial stability. The RBI has a paramount role to play and has acquitted itself creditably. He has outlined the evolution of monetary policy since the Bank's inception and delineates the relevant instruments employed. Monetary policy has been largely influenced by the changing paradigm in monetary economics and the developments in the financial markets and macroeconomic outcomes. Today we have the Board for Financial Supervision and the Board for Payment and Settlement Systems. The Financial Stability Unit conducts macro-prudential surveillance for financial system on an on-going basis. The RBI has evolved as one of the most respected institutions in India with the active support of the government.

This is a very useful and thought-provoking book with articles of a high calibre by outstanding experts in several fields. Space constraints has restricted us from covering all contributors.

•

Monetary Policy, Sovereign Debt and Financial Stability:
The New Trilemma
Edited by Deepak Mohanty
Published by Reserve Bank of India and Foundation Books;
Pages 370; Price ₹ 995

The RBI, as part of its non-traditional functions, has initiated a number of studies connected with our economy and held research conferences on global issues. In February 2012, the Bank organised the second international research conference on Monetary Policy, Sovereign Debt and Financial Stability: The New Trilemma.

The financial crisis that afflicted the globe and the resultant Eurozone sovereign debt crisis caused a sea-change in the science and art of central banking in a radical fashion. While central banking was concentrated on price stability through the short-term policy interest rate, it was assumed that price stability and macroeconomic stability would automatically ensure financial stability. This proved to be a costly assumption. Central banks are now faced with the new trilemma—simultaneous pursuit of price stability, sovereign debt sustainability and financial stability. The triple objectives reinforce one another and form a 'Holy Trinity' of objectives.

These issues were deliberated upon in the Second Conference and the book under review brings together the papers presented there. The RBI assembled veteran central bankers, academicians, policymakers, financial regulators and supervisors and private sector experts on a common platform in order to share their experiences. The volume has been edited by Deepak Mohanty, who is the Executive Director of RBI looking after monetary policy, economic research and statistics. He has immense experience of work in the IMF, where he was Senior Adviser. There are 15 contributors and 10 chapters. A number of chapters are dedicated to the challenges to monetary policy following the global crisis; whereas, few of them deal with issues relating to debt overhang. In a brief review, it will not be possible to cover all the chapters.

The keynote address of the Conference was delivered by Dr Subbarao, the former RBI Governor, who starkly poses the problem of "The Holy Trilemma". According to him, fiscal responsibility is more than a question of monetary policy independence—it is one of sustained economic stability. The government ought to leave responsibility to the regulators and assume an activist role only in the times of crisis. The Governor lays emphasis on communication in explaining the policy content.

The editor tackles the problem of efficacy of interest rate channel in monetary policy. His chapter presents an empirical evidence of such interest rate channels related to monetary policy transmission based on quarterly structural vector autoregressive (SVAR) framework. It incorporates the role of systemic liquidity in the modelling framework. Policy rate hikes have a negative impact on inflation with a lag of three quarters and the overall impact on inflation persists over 8-10 quarters.

Yung Chul Park, a Korean economist, examines the scope for macro-prudential policy in the context of emerging economies. There is a need to strengthen the foundation of the domestic financial system in order to improve its resilience to external shocks and to develop new policy instruments. He calls for better assessment of systemic financial risk and effectiveness of prudential controls of the supervisory agencies.

The chapter by Stephen G. Cechetti and Enisse Kharooubi—both economists from BIS—challenges the belief that finance is good for growth as it reduces transaction costs, raises investments directly and improves the distribution of capital and risk across the economy. With a sample of 21 AEs (advanced economies), the authors observe that faster growth in finance beyond a level is detrimental for aggregate real growth, and the financial booms are bad for trend growth. There is an increasing need to reassess the relationship of finance and real growth in modern economic systems.

Partha Shome, adviser to the Finance Minister, dissects the growth of public debt in AEs and demonstrates the spillover of the debt crisis into financial markets and examines the nature of measures taken by central banks. He advocates fiscal austerity through strong IMF surveillance to address the European sovereign debt crisis and policies aimed at containment of consumption in these economies.

Three authors—Barry Eichengreen, Eswar Prasad and Raghuram Rajan (present Governor of RBI) who outline the links obtaining in aspects of central banking argue that in the post-global financial crisis period, the exclusive focus on price stability by central banks has been challenged. Also, financial stability is no longer outside the direct ambit of monetary policy and cross-border spillovers have increased in scope and size and associated challenges for central banks. The three authors emphasise the need for an alternative framework in the post-crisis period. They have prepared a strategy for incorporating financial stability without diluting the objective of price stability. They underscore the role of macro-prudential tools to supplement the existing micro-prudential measures and regular meetings of central banks to assess policy implications.

This book is a refreshing and candid analysis of the challenges faced by countries, especially the emerging economies. The discussions are thorough and the volumes furnish a wealth of references both of books and articles from reputed international journals to which we may not have access. We must be thankful to the RBI for not only arranging such seminars, but also bringing out such valuable and easily assimilable publications.

Personalities

The RBI is not merely the foremost central bank among the developing countries; in its publications and researches, it is today a peer of the central banks of developed countries. Although it does not yet enjoy the autonomy in monetary and exchange matters that it deserves, it has the relevant technical expertise.

In the late 1940s and early 1950s, Dr J.V. Joshi, of Cambridge University and a student of John Maynard Keynes, was picked by C.D. Deshmukh as the economic adviser of the RBI. The research wing of the RBI had yet to develop. However, the RBI had stalwarts such as Dr P.S. Narayan Prasad and Dr B.R. Shenoy on its staff, which was later joined by Dr B.K. Madan, Professor S.L.N. Simha and Dr N.S.R. Sastry, among others.

By the mid- and late-1950s, the RBI had a strong research department with experts like Drs K.N. Raj, V.K. Ramaswamy, V.V. Bhatt, Chandavarkar, V.R. Cirvante, Khatkhate and several others. Dr K.N. Raj worked out the first detailed estimates, on the then modern methodology, of the balance of payments (BoP) of India for the immediate post-Independence years. The first technical report on money supply under the leadership of Prof Simha was presented. Dr V.V. Bhatt worked out the very first estimates of savings in India. Shri Chandavarkar made an estimate of liquidity supply in the Indian economy. The studies in the balance sheets of the private corporate sector also began. Debit to deposits studies were also commenced.

Here are interesting pieces on some of the RBI Executives and their related RBI stories.

Shri Abdul Kalam

The RBI family can be justifiably proud that one of its members has become the President of India. In the past, we had governors like Shri L.K. Jha and Dr C. Rangarajan being elevated to the posts of State Governors; but this was the first time that a Director on our Board had assumed the position of the country's first citizen. Dr Kalam's progress from Rameshwaram to Raisina Hill is akin to Abraham Lincoln's progress from Log Cabin to White House.

Dr Avul Pakir Jainulabdeen Kalam is the 11th Indian President. He was born in 1931 in Rameshwaram, son of a boat owner "who had neither much formal education nor much wealth." As a small boy he distributed newspapers, sold oil, onions, rice and novelties made of sea shells.

Dr Kalam has published his autobiography entitled *Wings of Fire* in association with Arun Tiwari who had worked under him for 10 years in the Defence Research and Development Organisation (DRDO) at Hyderabad. The book is a saga of a warm and intensely personal, deeply passionate story of a boat owner's son becoming India's most distinguished technocrat. It is also a brilliant account of the success story of India's Space Rocketry and Missile Programme.

Samuel Butler, a Victorian novelist wrote, "Greatness comes in the cloak of humility." No better description than this is possible of Dr Kalam. Two examples will elucidate this. In his autobiography, he writes with disarming candour that he was "...a short boy with rather undistinguished looks, born to tall and handsome parents. I ate with my mother. She would feed me on the floor of the kitchen, place a banana leaf before me, on which she ladled rice and aromatic sambhar...."

When Indira Gandhi summoned him to Delhi in 1980 so as to personally felicitate him for putting India on the world's space map, Dr Kalam was in a panic, as he owned neither a suit nor shoes. Prof

Satish Dhawan, his guru, and then Head of Indian Space Research Organisation (ISRO) told him, "You are beautiful clothed in your success."

His suit had been well earned. Under his guidance, India launched the first Satellite Launching Vehicle—the SLV-3. He also made the country a Missile power by developing the Agni and Prithvi. It is impossible to overestimate Dr Kalam's role in the 1988 Pokhran nuclear blasts—the result of 10 years of unremitting toil done by him and his team.

He aptly summarised his career thus—"my story is the story of a scientist tested by failures and setbacks; the story of a leader supported by a team of a dedicated professionals."

•

Shri A.G. Chandavarkar

Shri Anand Chandavarkar passed away on 19 September, 2011 in New York. He unarguably was the foremost exponent of the Indian economic scene and an acknowledged authority on John Maynard Keynes. He is noted for his grace in style, felicity of expression and profundity in knowledge. His credentials are impeccable. He was a graduate from the University of Bombay and the London School of Economics (LSE), where he was a student of Karl Popper and Michael Oakshott, two political philosophers of world repute. Greater distinction is that he was the disciple of three Nobel Laureates in Economics—Friedrich Hayek, James Meade and Ronald Coase. One cannot have more distinguished teachers. Then again, the teachers could not have a more distinguished disciple.

Professionally, he served in RBI, International Monetary Fund (IMF), Organisation for Economic Co-operation and Development (OECD) and World Bank; Economic Adviser, Bank of Libya; Consultant to the OECD (Paris), the World Bank, and the Presidential Commission on Finance and Banking, Sri Lanka.

Shri M. Narasimham, ex-Governor of RBI, in his gracefully written reminiscences *From Reserve Bank To Finance Ministry and Beyond* recalls the halcyon days of the Research Department of the RBI and the celebrated "Gang of Four" which included M. Narasimham, V.V. Bhatt, A.G. Chandavarkar and D.R. Khatkhate. These "Four Musketeers" rose to phenomenal heights occupying exalted positions in the world of banking, development and academia.

Chandavarkar was the author of *Keynes and India* and *Central Banking in Developing Countries*. His latest book was *The Unexplored Keynes and other essays*. He had published widely in leading academic and professional journals, including *The Economic Journal*, *The Oxford Economic Papers*, *The Quarterly Journal of Economics* and the *Economic and Political Weekly* (EPW). He made a significant contribution to *The Cambridge Economic History of India*.

He was an invited speaker at the Tenth Keynes Seminar at the University of Kent, Canterbury, England (1991) and the One Hundredth Annual Meeting of the American Philosophical Association, (Eastern Division), Washington D.C., 2003.

He is a rare economist, a profound scholar who writes with transparency and eloquence, and has many interesting things to say. His writings on Keynes are particularly fascinating and have attracted a huge readership. His deep knowledge regarding history of economics and economic analysis reflect the long and useful life he led as a teacher and researcher in the academic and international organisations. Shining through his writing is his compassion and humanity. Anand Chandavarkar displays his customary ability to "excite the judgment briefly rather than to inform it tediously." He is India's foremost and finest scholar of Keynes. His book, *Keynes and India* remains a classic.

He was a valuable contributor to the *EPW* and one cannot forget his articles on Keynes, Hayek, new structure of RBI, resignation of the first RBI Governor and many more.

He had worked in the Department of Research and Statistics of RBI for a number of years—in the 1950s and 1960s—and some of us were privileged to have worked under him. My wife and I had the fortune of visiting him in Washington and this 'Gentle Colossus' came down to the ground floor to see us off. In him, scholarship was combined with utmost courtesy, which one comes across rarely. We mourn the loss of a great scholar, a perfect gentleman and a raconteur par excellence.

He was 88 years old at the time of his death.

•

Shri S.L.N. Simha

S.L.N. Simha, a former Adviser of the Economic Department, staff member and Alternate Executive Director of the IMF passed away on 31 December 2008. He was 90 years old.

He served in several capacities, beginning his distinguished career as a University Professor, Adviser in Economic Department of RBI, General Manager in Industrial Development Bank of India (IDBI), Executive Director of the IMF, and Director of Institute of Financial Management, Chennai. He was also director on the boards of several public limited companies.

Simha's greatest work was the writing of the first volume of *History of RBI* relating to the period from 1935 to 1951—a magnum opus of almost 900 pages. This ensures him a niche in Indian banking history. He was the Founder Director of the Institute for Financial Management and Research. He headed this Institute from 1971 to 1980. Earlier, he worked as Alternate Executive Director in IMF; and on the occasion of the 50th anniversary of the IMF and the World Bank, he wrote a book, *Fifty Years of Bretton Woods Twins: IMF and World Bank* and he dedicated it to four Indian officials who had major roles in the founding and early years of both institutions: C.D. Deshmukh, J.V. Joshi, B.K. Madan, and P.S. Narayan Prasad—legendary names to old-time international monetary and financial officials.

A prolific writer, he wrote extensively on central banking, monetary policy, fiscal policy, and many economic topics. A pioneering study was his *The Capital Market of India*.

During his last years, Simha wrote a number of books of religious nature, such as, *Ramayana—The Glorious Epic*, English translations of *Mukundamala* (about Krishna), *Thiruppavai* (about Vishnu) and other works.

He was both student and Professor in Maharaja College, Mysore. Of interest is the fact that as a student, his benchmates were the Maharaja Chamaraja Wodeyar and Dr K.S. Krishnaswamy, later Deputy Governor.

On the birth centenary of H.V.R. Iengar, in a book released to felicitate him, Simha contributed an article where he wrote:

> HVR is an outstanding personality--brilliant as a student, extraordinarily competent, a very successful company chairman, a superb speaker--elegant without being ostentatious, clear, positive and compact. He was a master of the art of management, achieving results effortlessly with genuine enthusiasm for whatever he did.

Almost the same could be said of S.L.N. Simha.

Students and his several friends from the banking community will miss this tough and formidable, no-holds-barred banker whose contribution to RBI is truly memorable.

•

Dr Meenakshi Tyagarajan

Dr Meenakshi Tyagarajan was 88 years old when she passed away. She had retired in 1983 as Adviser, Department of Economic Analysis and Policy (DEAP). I can claim to have had the longest association with her in and out of the Bank. I knew her from the day she had joined DEAP.

The poet Wordsworth sang in his poem *The Prelude*:

> Bliss it was in the dawn to be alive
> But to be young was very heaven.

Those were the halcyon days of the Economic Department described accurately in two significant auto-biographical books. One is M.

Narasimham's *From Reserve Bank of India to the Finance Ministry and Beyond*; and the other is *Windows of Opportunity: Memories of an Economic Adviser* by Dr K.S. Krishnaswamy. Narasimham writes of the "Gang of Four" who dominated the Department—Dr V.V. Bhatt, Shri A.G. Chandavarkar, Dr D.R. Khatkhate and Shri M. Narasimham. Before them we had Dr K.N. Raj, Dr B.R. Shenoy, Dr Dharma Kumar, Shri D.S. Savkar and Shri V.G. Pendharkar.

It would not be wrong to say that "We Walked With Giants". Most of them wrote eloquently and passionately for the distinguished journal *EPW*, brilliantly edited by the legendary Krishna Raj with the active assistance of Dr K.S. Krishnaswamy.

Into this highly intellectual milieu, Meenakshi gently dropped in gravitating from a lecturer's post in Annamalai University. She had acquired a Doctorate from Kansas University in the United Sates (US). She used to be an important part of the Economic Department's intelligentsia and used to contribute to the monthly Bulletin, *Occasional Papers*. She wrote for several journals and of course for *EPW*. She was on the Board of Directors of a number of banks.

Her extracurricular attainments were formidable. No wonder! A peep into her lineage will convince you why.

Her grandfather, Madhaviah wrote the second–ever Tamil Novel, *Padmavathi Charitram*.

Her elder uncle was the Chief Justice of Madras—Justice M. Ananthanarayanan. He wrote a delightful English novel, *The Silver Pilgrimage*. About him, the American writer John Updike—a Pulitzer Prize winner—wrote a poem in the *New Yorker*—*I missed his book. I read his name.*

You should read that poem.

Another uncle was Shri M. Krishnan, the eminent wildlife expert—next only to Salim Ali. He was a good writer as well as sketch artist. His column, *Country Notebook* had begun in 1950 and was published continuously for 45 years in *The Statesman* of Calcutta.

Meenakshi was an affectionate person. Although she was posted to Bombay, she sought a transfer to Madras so as to look after her aged parents. She worked both in the Madras office and the Staff College. She was a very popular member of the Faculty in the College. When the College celebrated its Silver Jubilee, they asked her to write its biography.

She has written the biography of the first 25 years, *Reserve Bank Staff College—Evolution and Development*, which was released in 1989.

Kindly permit me one light diversion. Similar to the four queens in a pack of cards, we had during the 1960s and 1970s, four spinster queens in RBI—Kum Vimala Visvanathan, Kum Nalini Ambegaonkar, Kum I.T. Vaz and Kum Meenakshi Tyagarajan!

Meenakshi was a solidly built person, with a rough exterior but a heart of gold. The milk of human kindness oozed out of her and she was ever ready to help one and all. I was close to her as both of us were dedicated bibliophiles—bibliomaniacs! She and I were members of the British Council Library and the Asiatic Library. Hundreds are the books she has loaned to me or recommended.

I said Meenakshi was 88 years young! Not old. After her retirement, she lived in Chennai. Here she cultivated her interest in literature and Carnatic music. She translated into English her grandfather's book, *Padmavathi Charitram* as also the first ever Tamil novel—*Pratapa Mudaliar Charitram* by Mayuram Vedanayagam Pillai. She had written one more book on Tamil writers. The translations are highly accomplished and very well received. When I met her last March in her residence—a quaint bungalow named 'Meenakshi'—she was translating into English short stories written by her grandfather published in *The Hindu*—a 100 years ago! Grace of style and felicity of expression have been her forte.

Meenakshi had a puckish sense of humour. I will give three examples. The first is an extract from her biography of the Staff College (page 113).

Another source of discomfort is less amenable to correction. The battle against the "Mosquito Menace" has been waged more or less on a continuous basis, with pest control, spraying and, latest of all, the wire meshing of all windows. But the mosquitoes, for their part, improved their own training techniques to combat obstacles.

Second, during the Emergency years, we had Shri K.R. Puri as Governor. He brought as the Executive Director, Shri J.C. Luther who struck terror in every heart—well almost every heart. But not Meenakshi's. This was how she explained the situation: "Everyone is afraid of Luther but Luther is afraid of Menakshi. Well!. He saw my face once and it reminded him of a Battle Axe! And he kept a safe distance from me!"

Third, she has inscribed in all her books gifted to me—"To Pusthaka Puzhu Ramachandran"—meaning "Book Worm Ramachandran"— appellation I value highly.

•

Dr R.K. Hazari

Fame preceded the ensconcing into office of Dr R.K. Hazari, as the youngest Deputy Governor of RBI (he was in his late thirties). He had acquired recognition for his report on "Industrial Licensing Policy". He was highly informal and very popular. When I had bagged a prize in Hindi at an examination held by Government of India (GoI), the then Deputy Economic Adviser, Dr P.D. Ojha arranged for an award to be given by Dr Hazari. Thus, one evening all of us were received by the Deputy Governor (DG). He was told by Dr Ojha about the examination etc. Dr Hazari asked me pointedly, *"Main marwari hoon. Iska labh kya hai?"* I told him, *"Sir panch sau rupaye."* I added in English: "For me it is double honour to get this prize from my Guru." "Where did I teach you?", he asked. "I learnt Theory of Value for my MA, under you in Bombay University. You would come at 6 pm sharp, sit on an elevated chair, lecture on Hicks and Capital, every five minutes raising your right hand with a white chalk to the blackboard. But not a single day did you write a single word!" He laughed and said, "Even today at meetings my right hand moves up to an imaginary blackboard. All wonder. Only you know what it means."

Dr R.K. Hazari was the youngest Deputy Governor of RBI at only 37 years. He made a wonderful observation at the farewell to Shri M.S. Nadkarni, the then Chief Officer of Department of Banking Operations Development (DBOD).

> I was happy to note that when I took over as DG, I was having a Chief Officer who had as much experience in banking as I have lived in this world.

•

Dr V.V. Bhatt

Shri M. Narasimham, ex-Governor of RBI, in his gracefully written reminiscences, *From Reserve Bank To Finance Ministry and Beyond* recalls the halcyon days of the Research Department of RBI, and the celebrated "Gang of Four" which included M. Narasimham, V.V. Bhatt, A.G. Chandavarkar and D.R. Khatkhate. These "Four Musketeers" rose to phenomenal heights occupying exalted positions in the world of banking, development and academia. M. Narasimham wrote of Dr V.V. Bhatt: "...A soft-spoken person, an erudite scholar. And apart from being a first-rate economist, he had deep interests in philosophy. He could discuss, with equal felicity, capital coefficients and the subtler nuances of the verses of the Bhagavad Gita."

Dr Bhatt began his career as a lecturer in S.L.D. Arts College at Ahmedabad. He joined the RBI's Research Department in 1953 and continued until 1972 rising to the level of Adviser. Later on, he became Chief Executive of IDBI and thereon ascended to the prestigious of post of the Chief of Public Finance Division of the World Bank.

As a young student, Bhatt took part in Satyagraha organised by Gandhiji, was jailed for two months and lodged in the Sabarmati Jail. He went on to study at Harvard where he was taught by distinguished professors like Schumpeter and Wassily Leontiff.

After joining the Bank, Dr V.V. Bhatt started contributing several seminal articles on development to distinguished journals like *Economic Journal, Oxford Bulletin of Statistics,* and *Economia Internationale.* Most of these articles were published in a book, *Employment and Capital Formation in Underdeveloped Economies.* Dr Hannan Ezekiel, who was an economist with the IMF wrote about this book—"All the elements of development strategy of the second Five Year Plan were anticipated in the work done by Dr Bhatt in 1951-52."

At a seminar for young economists arranged by the International Economic Association and the Bombay School of Economics, several distinguished economists from all over the world took part—Joan Robinson, Nicholas Kaldor, Tarshis, Downie and others. Robinson and Kaldor paid a visit to RBI and conveyed to Governor Rama Rau their deep appreciation of the contribution of Dr Bhatt and hailed him as a star participant.

For three years, Dr Bhatt was the Chief Executive of IDBI where he laid the foundation for evolving criterion in regard to the evaluation of capital projects. During his term, he was deputed to Economic Commission for Asia and Far East (ECAFE) as a consultant and reviewed critically India's performance over the first two decades. This is published in a book entitled *Two Decades of Development: The Indian Experience.*

In September 1972, Dr Bhatt joined the Economic Development Institute of the World Bank. There he largely promoted two research projects—one on financial structures and policies for development and the other on management of public enterprises. These related to Philippines, Mexico and Brazil. Informal credit markets were also studied in respect of India and South Korea. During the decade ending 2000, Dr Bhatt served as an independent consultant to the World Bank. He prepared studies on countries such as Yemen, Ghana, Japan, Sri Lanka, etc.

His book of memoirs called *Perspectives on Development—Memoirs of a Development Economist* narrates the events in the formative period of

India's development process. As we look back, the band of economists like Dr Bhatt and his ilk (young economists working at a time our development process was in its nascent stage) stand tall in the roster of the researchers at RBI.

•

Shri R. Janakiraman
(My speech at his send-off function)

To be the third or fourth speaker at such a gathering is not exactly a happy position. No praises remain to be sung. No tributes remain to be paid. One runs the risk of repetition. Hence, I shall proceed on a slightly different track.

When I see this distinguished audience, my mind harks back to a historical occasion.

The Year: 1961
The Place: White House
The Room: Rose Room
The 35th President of the United States of America, John Fitzgerald Kennedy—the first US President of this century, born in this century—has one Camelot evening invited for dinner 17 Nobel Laureates, 23 Pulitzer Prize winners and 10 leaders of industry. Declared Kennedy, "This executive mansion has never seen such a gathering of brilliance, such a collection of talent except when Thomas Jefferson dined alone."

I am tempted to imitate the President and declare similarly that this executive building has never seen such a gathering of brilliance, such a collection of talent except when Sir Chintaman Deshmukh worked alone.

The occasion certainly deserves this magnificent response. Our beloved Deputy Governor Shri Janakiraman is bidding adieu to us all.

I wonder how many of you have noticed the sagacity with which his parents christened him. All of us have single names—Rama, Krishna,

Murali. His is a unique combination of two names—Janaki and Raman—signifying the cosmic union of the Male and the Female. The ancient Chinese called it "the Yang and the Ying" principle—symbolising compassion and love for the entire human race. Janakiraman has an abundance of both qualities.

Jayant Vishnu Narlikar, that eminent cosmologist in a recent review of the biography of Sir Isaac Newton wrote, "Newton's impact on science has been more comprehensive and far-reaching than that of any individual in History." In the words of the biographer, Richard Westfall, "Newton was one of the greatest scientists of all times, not one of the greatest but the greatest." After a long life studded with spectacular contributions to several fields, Newton was asked to assess his own contribution (perhaps an earlier version of our self-appraisal). He declared as follows: "I am a small child picking pebbles on the sea-shore. Before me lies the ocean of knowledge." We are all like small children on the sea-shore and without doubt persons like Janakiraman—Newtons of the banking world—tell us how to distinguish the pebble from the sand.

I shall refrain from waxing eloquent on the qualities of his head and heart. It is too universally known to re-iterate. He is head and shoulders over many stalwarts. He has carved for himself a niche—a Golden Niche—not only in the history of our Bank, but in our hearts as well.

I wish him a long, happy, scholarly retired life. He could, perhaps, write books after so many Reports. I pray that he maintains a close link with all of us.

I crave the indulgence of the Governor to bring to a close my tribute to Shri Janakiraman on a very light note. After Newton's gravity, a little levity. On this—the last day of Shri Janakiraman in RBI—I would like to take him back to his very first day in RBI. There is an utterly, butterly delightful story—its approbation is ever increasing and its currency ever widening. You, Sir, are reported to have appeared for your interview in a tuft—with a flower in it!

Is this story true or apocryphal? We would be pleased to be enlightened.

My best wishes to you, Sir.
P.P. Ramachandran

Note: The send-off function of R. Janakiraman attracted the maximum audience in any
function in RBI history. R. Janakiraman happily enough, began his response by saying,
"I am thankful to Ramachandran for taking me to my Day One in RBI..."

Episodes from My Diary

V.G. Pendharkar was the Alternate Executive Director of the IMF and World Bank, Member-Secretary of the Banking Commission, first Executive Trustee of Unit Trust of India (UTI), Executive Director of RBI, Director of the Export Credit-Guarantee Corporation of India (ECGC), Director of the Industrial Finance Corporation, Chairman of the Committee on the future of National Sample Survey Organisation (NSSO), Leader in Indian Delegation to ECAFE Conference on Asian Currency Union and Chairman of Working Group on the system of bank inspections. In addition to holding such highly coveted posts, he was appointed by the IMF as Adviser to the Bank of Tanzania.

Unlike the regular memoirs of a banker, Pendharkar's book, *Reminiscences of a Central Banker*, is a collection of anecdotes from his career in the country's central bank as well as in the Bank of Tanzania. He scrupulously keeps away from official history—for those interested, we have three hefty official volumes on the history of the RBI. The present work is replete with human interest stories. A few of these are worth recounting.

The author recalls Finance Minister Morarji Desai's visit to the Montreal Conference. B.K. Nehru and L.K. Jha—two Indian Civil Service (ICS) veterans—wanted to play a joke on the abstemious and upright Morarji. They took him to a nightclub. A hostess came and sat next to Morarji, naturally asking him whether he would like champagne. To which he replied, "I don't drink." Then she asked him, "What about a smoke?" And his answer was, 'I don't smoke." Annoyed at these answers, the hostess is reported to have retorted by saying,

Then you are not a gentleman. Morarji replied, "You are not a lady either." After some time, the floor show began. It was quite vulgar and Morarji got disgusted and returned to his hotel.

An interesting story is that of Nasser, President of Egypt. His government had approached the World Bank for a loan to build the Aswan Dam over the Nile river in order to control floods and ensure regular supply of water for irrigation. The American government wanted a guarantee from Nasser that Egypt would not attack the newly created state of Israel in return for its support to the proposal at the World Bank. Nasser was unwilling to give a guarantee and the World Bank turned down the proposal at US insistence. Nasser turned to Russia, which agreed to provide the necessary loan for an agreement to sell Egyptian cotton to Russia for 15 years. The Americans became jittery and sent Eugene Black to persuade Nasser, but the latter had already signed an agreement with Russia. Black returned with empty hands and a blackened face.

•

A Nugget From RBI "History"
All of us have been afflicted with old and soiled notes—especially those in Kerala and interior Maharashtra. All do not protest, but one did quite effectively.

Here is a letter written by a certain Akhileshwar and sent to Governor S. Jagannathan.

Read the full text and my comments at the end of this letter.

N. Akhileshwar,
9, Parekh Niwas, 135, Telang Road,
Matunga, Bombay-19

•

The Reserve Bank Governor
Bombay-1

Damn Your

You and your officers deserve to be shot dead for your bungling. For our convenience we bank our money in nearby banks. They give me soiled and torn notes. They say the money has been got from Reserve Bank. So they won't give good notes. If we go to shop or hotel, we cannot exchange the notes for our necessities. What the hell do you want me to do with the notes?. Neither the bank which gave me would accept them nor shopkeepers. So we have to come all the way to your stupid office and wait in queue?

Why the hell can't you withdraw old notes at source itself, i.e., in your office itself.

For your mismanagement, you should be given a garland of torn notes.

Sd/- N. Akhileshwar

•

It is a matter for joy that the letter did reach the highest authority, Governor Shri Jagannathan, who sent it on to the Finance Minister Y.B. Chavan, with his comments and recommendation—resulting in alleviation of the suffering. A word of praise is due to RBI for such meticulous maintenance of records and the gumption for sharing such a scurrilously written letter with the reading public.

P.P. Ramachandran

•

RBI Centenarian

On 27 March 2010, I had mailed a letter to Governor Dr D. Subbarao. Within hours of receipt, the Governor sent messages to the RDs at Chennai, Trivandrum and Kochi to co-ordinate and ensure that the felicitation of the centenarian Shri M.G. Nair is done. I am absolutely happy that today a team of four will leave Kochi to the house of Shri

Nair. As requested by me, they will gift Shri Nair a shawl, the RBI Platinum Jubilee Gold Coin and a bouquet for his wife.

Shri Nair is reasonably healthy and so is his wife too. The couple have 3 daughters, 6 grandchildren and 9 great-grandchildren. Shri Nair has worked in the Rangoon Office of RBI. One of his colleagues there was Shri Unni. It is heartening to note that this Rangoon Unni's son-in-law is part of the team to felicitate Shri Nair. He is Shri K.N.S. Unni, retired Adviser from Department of Economic Analysis and Policy (DEAP). In fact, it was Shri K.N.S. Unni who wrote to me six months ago about his meeting with the then 99 year old, Shri Nair. I thought it proper to honour this gentleman turning 100!

Shri Nair's daughter, Smt Kalyani Nair has retired from RBI, Chennai a few months ago.

For me, it is a matter of joy that the Governor of RBI took steps to accede to the request of an inconsequential retiree to honour a centenarian. I shall always cherish this act of the Governor and remain in his debt.

•

I had an occasion to review the latest book of Shri N.R. Narayana Murthy, *A Better India, A Better World*; he is also co-founder of Infosys. My review of this book can be seen elsewhere in this book.

He was for some years Director of the RBI Central Board.

Here are two extracts from his book of relevance to RBI. This deserves to be seen by all who work presently in RBI and also those who have retired.

> Several images pass through my mind, one after the other. Waiting at the entrance to the Reserve Bank of India month after month with my good friend Anil Bhatkal and sometimes with Sudha and little Akshara, for four to six hours, to obtain part of our own hard-earned dollars to support my six other founders, is an experience that I cannot forget and cannot wish on anyone else. (page 289)

If I wished to travel abroad even for a day, I had to make an application to the Reserve Bank of India (RBI) and wait for ten to twelve days. It was not always certain that I would get a positive response. I also had to submit a report on my trip abroad after I came back. A friend of mine was to travel to meet a few business prospects—a couple of them in Paris and one in Frankfurt. When he reached Paris, his second prospect asked him to meet him in Frankfurt since he had to leave for an urgent meeting there. The result was that my friend spent two days in Frankfurt and one day in Paris while the approval was for the reverse. When he returned to India and submitted his tour report to the RBI he was issued a 'show cause' notice as to why he should not be prosecuted for violating foreign exchange regulations!

Of course, things have become much easier today notes Narayana Murthy and writes, "We have the former RBI Governors Dr Bimal Jalan and Dr Y. Venugopal Reddy, two of our best free market champions, to thank for this." (page 87)